TAKING A STAND

PORTRAITS FROM THE SOUTHERN SECESSION MOVEMENT

By

Walter Brian Cisco

 WHITE MANE BOOKS

This White Mane Books publication
was printed by
Beidel Printing House, Inc.
63 West Burd Street
Shippensburg, PA 17257-0152 USA

In respect for the scholarship contained herein, the acid-free paper used in this book meets the guidelines for permanence and durability of the Committee on Production Guidelines for Book Longevity of the Council on Library Resources.

For a complete list of available publications
please write
White Mane Books
Division of White Mane Publishing Company, Inc.
P.O. Box 152
Shippensburg, PA 17257-0152 USA

Library of Congress Cataloging-in-Publication Data

Cisco, Walter Brian, 1947-
    Taking a stand : portraits from the southern secession movement /
  by Walter Brian Cisco.
        p.   cm.
    Includes bibliographical references and index.
    ISBN 1-57249-157-4 (alk. paper)
    1. Secession--Southern States.   2. Southern States--Politics and
  government--1775-1865.   3. United States--Politics and
  government--1815-1861.   4. United States--History--Civil War,
  1861-1865--Causes.   5. Confederate States of America--Biography.
  I. Title.
  E459.C57   1998
  973.7'13--dc21   98-41395
                                                                CIP

To my father and in memory of my mother

Contents

Illustrations

Preface

This is the story of the movement that led to Confederate independence, told from the perspectives of five participants. Chosen to illustrate various currents in the secession movement, each individual is the subject of a focused portrait. My aim in these sketches is to discover what led each man to abandon the Union.

In my account of Thomas Cooper and the first stirrings of secession I touch on some of the salient issues and personalities involved in American constitutional history. "Fire-eaters" — those radicals who embraced secession a decade or more before their peers — are well represented by the irrepressible Robert Barnwell Rhett. James Henley Thornwell shared the essential views and values of the Deep South's conservative majority. His conversion from American patriot to what historian James M. McPherson would call "pre-emptive counterrevolutionary" brings into focus the rationale behind formation of the Confederate States. Political control in the Upper South during 1860-1861 was in the hands of "anti-coercionists" — those who resisted secession until forced by Lincoln to choose between Union and their own vision of liberty. John Tyler and John Adams Gilmer typify the range of opinion among this pivotal group. In the epilogue we return to the opening scene — nearly four decades later — for the denouement.

Southern secessionists — vilified and stereotyped — are perhaps the most misjudged characters in American history. I hope that my approach, particularly in allowing these diverse but representative individuals to speak for themselves, will contribute to a fuller and fairer understanding of them and their cause.

This book was conceived and written as an introduction to the views of secessionists, not as a definitive investigation of antebellum thought or an exhaustive study of the causes of the War. It is by definition a Southern perspective. The opinions encountered may seem foreign to Americans raised on the facile dogmas and permitted conventions of popular history. Four million Americans did not march off to war in a political vacuum. Those who view the struggle over slavery as a morality play, as well as those who minimize slavery's importance, should both be challenged. In any case, I trust that readers will come to understand that the motivations of secessionists were complex and varied, their arguments eloquent, their explanations understandable and not illogical.

Napoleon is said to have dismissed history as "a set of lies agreed upon." We smile at his cynicism. Yet most of us must confess an inborn reluctance to question assumptions handed down to us about the past. Still, truth endures and is patient, if not necessarily kind. I am reminded of an item that appeared long ago in *Punch*, the London weekly of humor. "A cat, even if she be friendly, never approaches thee by a direct course," observed the anonymous wit. "No more does a truth, O friend; but winding round thy stupidities, and rubbing up against thy prejudices, it reaches thee gently — and then perhaps scratches."

I salute those helpful professionals at the University of South Carolina's South Caroliniana Library, Thomas Cooper Library, and University Archives; the Alderman Library, University of Virginia; the North Carolina Division of Archives and History; Duke University's Special Collections Library; the Manuscript Division, Library of Congress; and the Rush Rhees Library, University of Rochester. Not to be overlooked are the generous donors and long-suffering taxpayers who support many of these fine institutions.

I appreciate too the advice, help and encouragement of family and friends. Thanks are due Dr. Martin Gordon, Rev. Tom Anderson, David Cisco, Rod Gragg, Dr. John McGlone, Joyce Milkie and Harold Collier. Amanda and Steven deserve hugs for putting up with a dad who spends so much time in the past.

Walter Brian Cisco

Thomas Cooper

[A] government, whether ready made, to suit casual customers, or made to order, is the very last that operates as its framers intended. Governments are like revolutions: you may put them in motion, but I defy you to control them after they are *in* motion...

John Randolph of Roanoke[1]

Calculating the Value of the Union
Thomas Cooper

In the summer of 1827 there were still a few old-timers who could recall when fields and forests belonging to James and Thomas Taylor covered the high ground east of the Congaree River. South Carolina legislators, meeting in Charleston just five years after the winning of American independence, had bowed to the growing strength of the upcountry by choosing this site near the center of the state and ordering a new capital be built. It was a bold and farsighted plan. Broad streets, some as much as one hundred and fifty feet wide, were laid out in a grid covering four square miles and soon a village appeared amid the pine trees. A modest wooden capitol building was erected in the center. After briefly considering "Washington" for the new town's name, lawmakers finally settled on "Columbia."[2]

With an economy tied to state government and cotton, Columbia had by her fourth decade grown to a town of just over three thousand residents, some four hundred homes and several score businesses. All of the major Christian denominations had their own houses of worship, and a number of academies welcomed young scholars. Columbians were proud of the canal that had recently been dug to bypass the rocks and shallows of the Congaree, an improvement that allowed boats carrying 45,612 bales of cotton to pass down river in the year of 1827 alone. The State Road led from Columbia to the seaport metropolis of Charleston, though travelers complaining of high tolls often searched out the free roads. Stagecoaches connected the capital with Charleston, Camden, Augusta and Greenville.

Spanning the river at Gervais Street was a new covered bridge, resting on piers of granite, one thousand three hundred and fifty feet long. A "street railroad," powered by a team of horses, carried passengers and freight from the canal up Gervais, turning down Richardson Street into the main business district. At the northeastern boundary of town stood the new Insane Asylum, architect Robert Mills' masterful blend of practicality and pleasing Greek symmetry. Just off Sumter Street the plain brick structures of South Carolina College rose above a tree-shaded campus. Nearby was the State House, capitol of South Carolina. Though handsomely furnished and adequate for the needs of the present, a more imposing edifice was already on the minds of many.

Dominating the steeples and rooftops of downtown Columbia, from the corner of Richardson and Washington Streets, was Town Hall. Gentlemen set their gold pocket watches by the hands of the great clock in the tower. At night a lookout from his lofty perch scanned the darkness, searching for flames, ready to awaken fire crews by a wild ringing of the tower's bell. He routinely sounded the bell on the hour, and on the half-hour was required to cry out, "All is well!" assuring townsfolk that their guardian was still awake. The building's upper floor, reached by outside stairs, was Town Hall proper, where intendant and wardens of the council met. Open to the unpaved streets through archways, the lower level was occupied by a public market. Here was the very heart of Columbia where, shaded from the summer sun, people could buy fresh meat and vegetables, or simply gossip and argue the issues of the day.

The hottest topic of political conversation this June was the new tariff bill pending before the United States Congress. Another in a series of increasing import duties, this one designed to protect domestic woolen production, the proposal was bitterly condemned throughout the state. The *Telescope*, Columbia's weekly newspaper, carried a story of a protest meeting in Walterboro that declared the proposed tariff to be "in opposition to our constitutional rights." A resolution put forward at a meeting of the Charleston Chamber of Commerce characterized the bill as "an aggravation of an already unequal and burthensome tax on the consumption of the southern states." Port City merchants went on to warn that such discriminatory legislation could only foster "a spirit of disaffection that may come to regard the federal charter with alienated feelings."[3]

The people of Columbia too were anxious to be heard. At first the intendant called a public meeting for Friday, June 29, but then postponed it until the following Monday in order to permit those living at a distance to attend. "We hope there will be but one voice on this vitally important subject," editorialized the *Telescope* in publicizing the gathering. An unnamed "Subscriber" submitted to the newspaper, and they published, a long list of resolutions to be formally offered at the meeting. Not for this hotspur the restrained rhetoric of Charleston's business community. Protectionism he denounced as a scheme "plainly calculated to make one section of the union tributary to another." Inevitably the question must, in his view, be confronted: "[I]n what manner are the southern states benefited by the union?"[4]

Raised windows and fluttering fans did little to relieve the oppressive afternoon heat, but Town Hall was filled as the meeting came to order at three. South Carolina Governor John Taylor had been asked to preside as chairman, with Professor Henry J. Nott serving as secretary. Speaking first, in the major address of the afternoon, would be sixty-seven-year-old Thomas Cooper, president of South Carolina College.[5]

Less than five feet tall, with a massive bald head, one student described Cooper as "a perfect taper from the side of his head down to his feet; he looked like a wedge with a head on it." The college boys laughingly nicknamed him "Old Coot," perhaps because he reminded them of a terrapin. The preposterous figure of President Cooper astride his old white mule named "Blanche" was a common sight as he rode about town.[6] Yet few in the audience this day had ever heard him speak. Fewer still knew anything of his background.

———

From the first there was little about the life of Thomas Cooper that could be called predictable. Born in Westminister, England in 1759, young Mr. Cooper enjoyed the advantages of a well-to-do family, even as he disappointed his father by dropping out of Oxford University. While still in his teens he married a girl named Alice Greenwood. Yet somehow he found time to study both law and medicine, eventually practicing in both fields, even as he developed what would become a lifelong interest in chemistry.

After 1785 Cooper lived near the booming textile center of Manchester.[7] It was here he first entered the political fray and soon became a thorn in the side of the local establishment. As a member of the Manchester Constitutional Society he argued that universal manhood suffrage and frequent elections would make Parliament more representative. Many of his Tory opponents no doubt feared he was right. Cooper battled state support of the Church of England and all government-imposed religious restrictions, and though claiming to accept the authority of the Bible, in truth felt most comfortable with Unitarianism. Friendship with liberal theologian Joseph Priestly no doubt influenced his views.[8]

Stirred by the prospects for liberty in revolutionary France, Cooper and several associates visited Paris in the turbulent spring of 1792. France tottered on the brink of a second bloody revolution as Jacques Pierre Brissot's Girandists cried out for war against Austria. Amid the excitement Cooper and his friends appeared before the Jacobin Club as representatives of the Manchester group and there pledged solidarity with

Maximilien Robespierre's society as "the most determined enemies of arbitrary power." This was too much for Edmund Burke. The Whig philosopher-statesman upbraided Cooper before the House of Commons, forcing the Constitutional Society to disavow any association with French extremism, pleading that they merely wished to restore the British Constitution "to its original purity." Cooper himself was not so easily cowed. On his return from France he launched a counteroffensive, lashing out against Burke in an eighty-page pamphlet. Cooper's enthusiasm for the French experiment would soon cool, and by the time the reign of terror came he had lost faith in the revolution, the noble words and slogans swept away by a "ferocious injustice of many of their practices."[9]

Cooper suffered no real persecution for his radical pronouncements, but his friend Priestly's home was torched by an angry mob. The pioneering chemist had been an outspoken supporter of revolution in France. The Constitutional Society protested the outrage, but Cooper's bitterness only deepened. As change in British society and government seemed hopeless, both he and Priestly determined to make new lives in America. The thirty-three-year-old Cooper left for the new land in 1793 with his older children, returning the next summer to gather up his wife and smaller offspring, having chosen Pennsylvania for their new home.[10]

Settling in Northumberland, Cooper supported his family by the practice of law, lived for a time with Priestly, and for a few months edited the Sunbury and Northumberland *Gazette*. Describing himself as a "decided opposer of political restrictions on Liberty of the Press, and a sincere friend of those first principles of republican Government," his editorial output was soon republished in book form.[11] In a few years outspoken opposition to President John Adams would bring him into conflict with the notorious Sedition Act.

In 1801 Cooper was appointed to chair a state commission charged with settling longstanding land disputes in Luzerne County. It was experience that served him well when a new judicial district was formed in this same area and he was appointed state judge. About this time Cooper began speaking out in favor of free trade, a stand that could not help but make powerful enemies in Pennsylvania. He was willing to grant that tariffs provided necessary income and even to concede that protectionism itself might at times be justified in the name of national defense. But a permanently high tariff designed to profit manufacturers at the expense of consumers was, in Cooper's view, patently unfair and unconstitutional. Merchants he denounced as "a swinish multitude," ready to risk even war for their own selfish interests.

Political and personal enemies conspired in 1811 to remove Cooper from the bench. He turned to teaching, first at Carlisle (now Dickinson) College and later at the University of Pennsylvania, supplementing a meager income by writing and editing. During these years Cooper carried on an extensive correspondence with Thomas Jefferson, sharing views on a wide range of topics. The former president held Cooper to be "the greatest man in America, in the powers of mind, and in acquired information," and hoped that a professorship could be arranged for him at the soon-to-be-opened University of Virginia.[12] Cooper would wait years for an offer that never came, finally taking a position teaching chemistry at South Carolina College.

When Cooper first decided on emigrating to America he had ruled out making a home in the South because of his distaste for slavery. Though never an abolitionist, as a young man he wrote forcefully against the slave trade. Then as the years passed he began to take a hard look at some of the earlier tenants of his political faith. A growing conservatism, nurtured by experience, gradually transformed the uncomplicated idealism of youth. "Rights," he came to conclude, "are what society acknowledges and sanctions, and they are nothing else." He would become one of the first to boldly defend rather than apologize for slavery, arguing that it was a universal human institution, sanctioned even by scripture and beneficial to both master and slave. As soon as Cooper arrived in Columbia he purchased two black families, and thereafter accepted without qualm the American South's "peculiar institution."[13]

At first he preferred to think of the South Carolina teaching job as temporary, still hoping to hear from authorities at the University of Virginia. By April of 1820, despairing of ever receiving an offer from that school, he accepted as permanent the post in Columbia and took on the additional tasks of teaching geology and mineralogy. South Carolina College President Jonathan Maxcy died in June. The trustees quickly picked a replacement, but when he declined they turned to their chemistry professor and elected him president pro tempore. The following year Cooper was narrowly elected South Carolina College's second president, a position he would fill for a dozen years.

He soon developed a reputation for being unable to maintain discipline on campus, though in fairness his predecessor and successors did little better. He often complained to Jefferson of his unruly students and their touchy sense of pride. "Republicanism is good," he concluded, "but the 'rights of boys and girls' are the offspring of Democracy gone mad." Cooper tried unsuccessfully to have South Carolina College made a tuition-free institution. He used his influence and abilities to promote the establishment of a medical college in the state, advocated additional funding for South Carolina's few public schools and worked hard for improved care and treatment of the mentally ill.[14]

President Cooper diligently attended chapel services at the college, sat with his family in the Episcopal church on Sundays and for the most part refrained from disturbing the religious upbringing of his students. Until they were grown, "they ought to follow the religion of their parents."

Student James Henley Thornwell remembered the boys once asking that classes be canceled because the governor had proclaimed a day of fasting. "The Doctor replied," said Thornwell, "that the part of the commandment enjoining six days labour, was as obligatory as that which directed the keeping holy of the Sabbath." Still, Cooper's outspoken deism drew the orthodox clergy into what became a running battle. Political foes no doubt encouraged scrutiny of his irreligion as their best hope of ridding the state of his influence. For if Cooper remembered to guard his tongue when speaking to students on religious topics, he was unrestrained in his political evangelism. He advocated the most advanced states' rights position of the day, going so far as to call himself an "anti-Federalist." While president he continued to teach several courses, including one of the first in political economy offered in America. His laissez-faire economic theories and faith in state sovereignty would profoundly influence an entire generation of the state's leaders. In the classroom and out, he was a spellbinding raconteur. One student recalled how Cooper "had mingled intimately with the most remarkable men of the old and new world...With wonderful art, he could weave a dinner with Priestly, a glass of wine with Robespierre, a supper with the Brissotians...into a lecture upon asbestos, soda, or magnesia." "He was rarely in a company," remembered a friend, "in which he did not say the best thing that was uttered."[15]

━━━━━━━━

All eyes in the hot and crowded Columbia Town Hall were fixed on the familiar form of Doctor Cooper as he rose to speak. His opening words seemed conventional enough, proposing formally that the resolutions published the previous Friday in the local newspaper be adopted. He then proceeded to quote several reports of new manufacturing industries demanding protection, all designed "permanently to force upon us a system, whose effect will be, to sacrifice the south to the north, by converting us into colonists and tributaries..." An onerous tax had replaced the modest revenue duties originally imposed. And now the manufacturing interests, concentrated as they were in the towns and cities and far better organized than farmers and planters, have "a drilled and managed majority" in the House of Representatives.

The last presidential election had been decided in the House, where John Quincy Adams triumphed when Henry Clay threw his support to this eldest son of John Adams. Now Clay, that "manufacturer of Presidents," came in for Cooper's special invective. Clay's advocacy of high protective tariffs, a national bank and federally-funded roads and canals offered little to Southern agriculturalists who were expected to pay the bills. That Clay chose to label his scheme "the American System" only added insult to economic injury. The manufacturers desired nothing less than a plan "by which the earnings of the south are to be transferred to the north." Southern tillers of the soil under this mis-named "American System" are to be subservient to "the master minds of Massachusetts, the Lords of the spinning-jenny, and Peers of the power loom!"

Cooper said that he wished manufacturers well and, all other considerations being equal, preferred to do business with American enterprises. But there must be no special advantages granted. "If he cannot make goods as cheap and of as good quality," argued Cooper, "is that a reason why his deficiencies should be made good out of our pocket, by compelling us to pay exorbitant prices?" Congress had a right to regulate commerce, but nothing in the Constitution could justify the gross inequities of the protective system, a provocation to foreign nations that was bound to result in retaliation.

No one was prepared for the thunderclap about to explode in the hall and reverberate across the country. The printed resolutions had carried a hint, asking for a sober consideration of just how much the Southern states were benefited by their union with economic interests so different from their own. In his conclusion Cooper returned to that point.

"I have said, that we shall ere long be compelled to calculate the value of our union; and to inquire of what use to us is this most unequal alliance? by which the south has always been the loser and the north always the gainer? Is it worth our while to continue this union of states, where the north demand to be our masters and we are required to be their tributaries? Who with the most insulting mockery call the yoke they put upon our necks the AMERICAN SYSTEM! The question however is fast approaching to the alternative, of submission or separation."

Professing to hope that reason might yet prevail he proffered an olive branch, only to cast it down as if it were a gauntlet. "Most anxiously would every man who hears me wish on fair and equal terms to avoid it. But, if the monopolists are bent on forcing the decision upon us, with themselves be the responsibility. Let us however apply to the feelings of truth and justice, and patriotism among our fellow citizens, while there are hopes of success. I would fain believe it is not yet in vain. But at all events we must hold fast to *principle*: if we compromise our *rights*, and act from motives of expediency we trust to a broken anchor, and all that is worth preserving will be irretrievably lost."[16]

II.

One day in May of 1794 John Taylor, forty-year-old senator from Virginia, was interrupted as he walked down a corridor in the United States capitol in Philadelphia. Taylor recognized New York's Federalist Senator Rufus King motioning him into a deserted committee room. King seemed agitated. Once the door closed and they were alone he came right to the point. The Union, said King, must be dissolved. The economies of the North and South are incompatible, making a political separation inevitable. Only a peaceful dissolution of the United States, King concluded, could avert a violent breakup.

While King was presenting his case the door swung open and in walked Connecticut Senator Oliver Ellsworth. The New Englander at once seconded King's proposal and pleaded for Taylor's help in bringing about a friendly parting of the ways between the sections.

An astonished Taylor quickly replied that should the Union be divided he certainly preferred it to be peaceful, but that he had not given up hope. Grievances and disparate interests, insisted Taylor, could yet be reconciled and the Union preserved.

No, complained King, sectional differences were too profound. Soon, he feared, the South would grow to become the majority section, a state of affairs that the people of the Northeast would never tolerate. Only a dissolution of the Union now, by the mutual consent of both parties, could avert disaster.[17]

There the matter would remain for the time being. If Taylor was shocked by the apostasy of his political opponents he could not help but smile at the irony of the moment. Both King and Ellsworth had been members of the Constitutional Convention and ardent advocates of a new and stronger union. Taylor had raised his voice against Virginia's ratification of the Constitution, preferring the Articles of Confederation or even the independence of the Old Dominion to that closer bond of union pressed by the victorious party.[18]

Taylor's political philosophy was essentially that of the revolutionary generation, cherishing individual liberty and keeping a wary eye on government. Particularly to be distrusted was centralized authority. Love of liberty had motivated Englishmen like Algernon Sidney to battle against both the hereditary power of monarchs and the dictatorship of Cromwell. A century after his martyrdom under Charles II, Sidney's vision of republican liberty found wholehearted acceptance in America. Taylor could identify too with those English libertarians who saw public-spirited virtue in an agrarian lifestyle, corruption and potential tyranny in the wealth and power of London. "Power is like Fire," said Englishman Thomas Gordon in 1721, "it warms, scorches, or destroys, according as it is watched, provoked, or increased. It is as dangerous as it is useful." Fellow libertarian John Trenchard warned of "wicked ministers" conspiring to use war, party strife and immorality to control the people. Should the constitution get in their way, "then must the Constitution itself be attacked and broken, because it will not bend." A tension between "country" and "court" would cross the Atlantic to become a recurring theme in American public affairs.[19]

Born in Caroline County in 1753, Taylor attended a boarding school with young James Madison and later studied at the College of William and Mary. He was admitted to the bar in 1774 only to have his law career postponed by the outbreak of the revolutionary war. When his uncle,

Edmund Pendleton, was elected to the Second Continental Congress Taylor accompanied him to Philadelphia. There, in the aftermath of Lexington and Concord, the young Virginian was caught up in the excitement of the independence movement. Returning home in the company of his uncle and Patrick Henry, Taylor quickly secured a commission in the 2nd Virginia Regiment and by 1777 was serving in the Continental Army with the rank of major and had seen action at Brandywine Creek in Pennsylvania. But two years of inactivity followed and Taylor resigned, re-established his law practice and sought election to the Virginia House of Delegates. [20]

Having lost the initiative in the Northern colonies, the British determined to salvage at least something of their American empire by an offensive in the South. Georgia and South Carolina became a major theater of war and by 1780 Virginia was suffering the depredations of turncoat General Benedict Arnold. Virginia patriots began complaining of a lack of Northern support during their time of trouble. Penned by Taylor, Patrick Henry and John Tyler, Sr., the Virginia legislature made a formal protest to Congress in 1781. Southerners had hurried to the aid of their Northern brethren, ran the argument, when war raged on their territory. "But when we come to look for our Northern allies, after we had thus exhausted our powers in their defense," scolded the Virginians, "they were not to be found..."[21]

With or without their Northern compatriots victory at Yorktown was within sight. The war would end with Taylor again in uniform, commanding a militia "legion" with the rank of lieutenant colonel. Rather than run for re-election Taylor returned to the practice of law, invested in land and eventually developed three prosperous plantations. He confessed to "a spice of fanaticism in my nature upon two subjects—agriculture and republicanism," and set to work making his plantations models of efficiency. He wrote extensively of his agricultural practices, encouraging a steady stream of visitors determined to learn more of his secrets. And that "spice of fanaticism" in the cause of republican liberty would not allow him to stay out of the political arena. He returned to his seat in the Virginia legislature, styling himself "John Taylor of Caroline" to distinguish himself from a Southhampton County lawmaker of the same name.[22]

John Taylor of Caroline found much to be proud of in the American Confederation. In the 1780s nine out of ten Americans lived on farms, and agricultural exports by the end of the decade had doubled from pre-war levels. The war itself had encouraged manufacturers and their production continued to grow with the coming of peace. Even after prosecuting a long war the national debt was but twelve dollars per capita and Congress was preparing to retire this obligation through the sale of Western lands. Still, complaints could be heard.

The articles established a confederacy in which "Each state retains its sovereignty, freedom and independence, and every Power, Jurisdiction and right, which is not by this confederation expressly delegated to the United States, in Congress assembled." The struggle for independence had been directed by the Continental Congresses, essentially revolutionary bodies, and not until final ratification of the articles in March 1781 did all thirteen states agree to this new and "perpetual union." Though Congress's expressed powers were extensive, the approval of nine of the thirteen states was required to pass legislation, each state casting one vote. Enforcement of laws depended largely on the cooperation and willingness of the states themselves since no federal executive or judicial branches existed. It was up to the states to raise revenue needed by the Confederation, and in this they were predictably lax. Congress was unable to regulate commerce. Amendments required the unanimous approval of the states.[23]

Pressure began to build for some sort of alteration, replacement of the articles or perhaps even more radical remedies. One idea beginning to be discussed was that of breaking up the United States into three mini-confederacies, made up of the New England, Middle and Southern states. There had been talk back in 1775 among delegates to the Second Continental Congress of forming "two grand Republics," North and South, recognition even then of sectional divergence. By 1787 Madison expressed astonishment that dismemberment of the Union, "after long confinement to individual speculations and private circles, is beginning to show itself in the Newspapers."[24]

In a world of monarchies and despotisms the republican experiment in America was closely watched. Benjamin Franklin feared that a weak and ineffectual federal government would encourage the enemies of liberty everywhere to gloat "that popular Government cannot long support themselves." The concerns of George Washington echoed those of Franklin. Unless more power was granted to Congress, warned the general, the people might in desperation turn to a "monarchical form of Government." Such a failure would be "a triumph for the advocates of despotism to find that we are incapable of governing ourselves..." During the revolutionary war Alexander Hamilton had urged Congress, as yet unfettered by a constitution, to use its "undefined powers" to do whatever it thought necessary to win independence. He frankly desired a "solid, coercive union" possessing "complete sovereignty." The army was an "essential cement of the union," according to Hamilton, and Congress should go to any length to secure its loyalty. Sam Adams could only shake his head at that kind of reasoning. Soldiers of a standing army, in contrast to local militiamen, "are apt to consider themselves as a body distinct from the rest of the citizens," therefore a dangerous weapon in the wrong hands. "Such a power," concluded Adams, "should be watched with a jealous eye." The adoption of the Articles of Confederation had been a victory for those with "a jealous eye" on congressional power, but the specter of consolidation refused to die. A committee of what might be termed "nationalists" submitted an amendment to the articles that would have armed Congress with the power of the military to enforce its will on the states. When that proved impossible to sell, the same group grumbled that Congress should simply exercise whatever powers it thought proper, ignoring legal restraints.[25]

Finally came a fit call for action. A 1786 meeting of state delegates in Annapolis, there to discuss the regulation of commerce, ended with members asking that a convention be held in Philadelphia the following May. Using the most general of terms, since as yet no consensus existed as to what changes should encompass, this proposed convention was charged with formulating a plan to revise the constitution. One by one states began choosing delegates and, not to be left out, Congress belatedly bestowed its blessing.[26]

Near the end of May delegates representing a quorum of states had gathered in the Philadelphia State House and there began their deliberations. "Let us raise a standard to which the wise and honest can repair," said convention president George Washington. "The event is in the hand of God." Meeting in secrecy in order to avoid igniting premature controversy, members quickly decided to create a new fundamental law rather than try to repair the old articles. For the time being the convention concluded "that provision ought to be made for the continuance of a Congress," but there seemed to be an assumption among delegates, and in the state legislatures, that by convening a constitutional convention the old Confederation had in effect gone out of business. Though Congress would continue to hold sessions in New York City, by common consent the "perpetual union" had slipped quietly into a sort of limbo.[27]

Most delegates came to Philadelphia convinced that a government was needed possessing executive and judicial powers, as well as legislative. Agreement ended there. Considered first was the "Virginia Plan," put forward by the largest and most populous state, calling for a more powerful Congress elected by popular vote. "New Jersey will never confederate on the plan before the committee," warned delegate William Paterson. "She would be swallowed up." Little Rhode Island was so fearful of being "swallowed up" that she refused even to be represented at the convention. Delegates from the small states preferred the "New Jersey Plan," essentially a revision of the articles, under which each state retained equal representation in Congress. Ultimately only the "Great Compromise" — representation by population in the House of Representatives and equal representation by states in the Senate — kept delegates from walking out. Nationalists were bitterly opposed to state equality in the upper chamber, as that implied state sovereignty, but went along out of sheer necessity. So important to the small states was their equal vote in the Senate that it became the one provision the Constitution itself declared forever unalterable.[28]

Never considered was Hamilton's proposal to replace the states with an all-powerful central government dominated by a ruler chosen for life. Hamilton, in the words of a Connecticut delegate, is "praised by every body...supported by none." But arguments among delegates over the question of sovereignty — ultimate political power — probably changed no minds. Luther Martin of Maryland held that the former colonies acquired sovereignty as states when they declared independence in 1776. No, insisted Hamilton, the step was taken by the states united, not individually. The wording of the Declaration, proclaiming "That these United Colonies are, and of Right ought to be Free and Independent States," seemed unambiguous. The 1783 treaty of peace with Great Britain listed all thirteen states individually, "His Britannic Majesty" acknowledging each to be "free, sovereign and independent." Rufus King went on to claim that the states in joining together in a confederacy had given up "essential portions" of their sovereignty. Martin argued that in calling the convention the states had reverted to their sovereign, pre-Confederation status. When at one point it was proposed that Congress be granted the power to "call forth the force of the Union" against any state found to be at odds with the federal government, James Madison quickly moved that the proposal be postponed and it was never voted upon. To march federal troops against a state "would look more like a declaration of war than an infliction of punishment," predicted Madison, "and would probably be considered by the party attacked as a dissolution of all previous compacts by which it might be bound." Even the most extreme nationalists could also see how such a provision would continue to define the Union as a league of states, however draconian the demands for obedience.[29]

A North-South cleavage was obvious in the debate over how slaves should be counted when it came to apportioning representation in the House of Representatives. Since 1780 five states north of the Mason-Dixon Line had abolished slavery or taken steps toward ending it. Elbridge Gerry of Massachusetts, representing a state that had recently freed its few bondmen, argued that slaves were no more than property and therefore should not be numbered as population. Under the articles slaves had been counted at three-fifths of their whole number when apportioning a state's financial obligation to the Confederation. Charles Pinckney of South Carolina suggested that the old formula be followed in the new Constitution's rule for representation, and his motion carried. Another "sectional" issue was resolved by a Pinckney compromise when delegates from slave-trading New England joined forces with four Southern states to extend the trade until 1808. Had there been any "intention...to touch slavery," said Pinckney, "no Constitution would have been achieved."[30]

One of the convention's last acts was to send the draft of the Constitution to a "Committee of Style" in order to polish the work. As originally written and approved the Preamble began, "We the people of the states of," and proceeded to list all thirteen members of the old Confederation, including unrepresented Rhode Island. Since the approval of just nine states would put the new Constitution into effect among those ratifying it, and as the assent of all thirteen was anything but assured, the Committee of Style thought it prudent to simply shorten the phrase to "We the people of the United States." That shortened phrasing, and a few innocuous words of introduction, were approved without debate or objection by the convention.[31] Only later would polemists profess to see broad meaning and justification for nearly unlimited federal activity in the Preamble's poetry.

The proposed Constitution went to the states for ratification and immediately was attacked for not containing a list of guaranteed fundamental rights. Supporters of the Constitution, calling themselves "Federalists," countered with the argument that since the new government would be one of strictly limited powers, a bill of rights would be superfluous. The federal government will be confined, wrote Madison even before the Tenth Amendment was penned, "to certain enumerated objects." To attempt a list of rights might even encourage the misconception that a right not listed did not exist. "[W]ho will be bold enough," asked James Wilson, "to enumerate all the rights of the people?" Still, the Constitution's failure to include a bill of rights proved difficult for supporters to explain.[32]

Patrick Henry, opponent of ratification, envisioned federal authorities "laying what taxes they please, giving themselves what salaries they please, and suspending our [state] laws at their pleasure." Other anti-Federalists charged that the new Constitution would establish a government federal in some ways and national in others, but inevitably the tendency would favor consolidation. They were ever mindful that republican institutions required tender care and ceaseless vigilance in order to survive. Government must remain small and close to those governed. Freedom was impossible without a virtuous people agreed on fundamental values. They accepted the traditional view, therefore, that a single republic extending over a vast area was unthinkable. Consolidation they equated with the death of freedom.[33]

Hamilton only scoffed at their fears. "The moment we launch into conjectures about the usurpations of the federal government," chided Hamilton, "we get into an unfathomable abyss, and fairly put ourselves out of the reach of all reasoning." Opponents of the Constitution in Pennsylvania expressed apprehension over congressional control of each states' citizen-soldiers. "The militia of Pennsylvania," they feared, "may be marched to New England or Virginia to quell an insurrection occasioned by the most galling oppression, and aided by the standing army, they will no doubt be successful in subduing their liberty and independency..." Hamilton would ridicule such talk as "exaggerated and improbable."

Madison, also pressing for ratification, took the concerns of anti-Federalists more seriously. "In the contest with Great Britain," he pointed out, "one part of the empire was employed against the other. The more numerous part invaded the rights of the less numerous part." But if such a "trial by force" were to be held in the new union he was confident that massive resistance would render the attempt impossible. Madison emphasized the federal character of the new charter, pointing out that ratification "is to be given by the people, not as individuals composing one entire nation, but as composing the distinct and independent States to which they respectively belong." Ratification or rejection of the new Constitution was the choice of sovereign states, acting individually. "In this relation," he concluded, "the new Constitution will, if established, be a *federal*, and not a *national* constitution."[34]

Should the Union fail and there be a "dismemberment of the empire," in Hamilton's words, he projected two confederacies eventually arising in America — North and South. Because of "geographical and commercial considerations, in conjunction with the habits and prejudices of the different States," a hypothetical Southern confederacy would likely adopt free trade policies. His words were meant to be taken as a warning to New York, added reason to ratify the Constitution and keep all the states under one government. Down in Virginia anti-Federalists pointed to possible Northern economic domination in their arguments against the new union. William Grayson feared that the North, having too little in common with the South, would gain the upper hand "and every measure will have for its object their particular interest." His concern was echoed by Patrick Henry who charged that the proposed government "subjects everything to the northern majority." For Virginia to join this union would "put unbounded power over our property in hands not having a common interest with us." Federalist James Innes downplayed the threat, asking if a Northern-dominated government would be so foolish "as to alienate the affections of the Southern States, and adopt measures which will produce discontents, and terminate in a dissolution of a union as necessary to their happiness as to ours?" Another Virginia Federalist reasoned that ratification should proceed because, contrary to expectations, the South might someday re-emerge as the majority section. "A very sound argument indeed," mocked George Mason, "that we should cheerfully burn ourselves to death in hopes of a happy resurrection!"[35]

The Virginia Convention would eventually ratify, despite the passionate oratory of a distinguished anti-Federalist minority, by a vote of 89 to 79. Yet in the very act of ratification delegates made it clear that they were yielding only those powers specifically enumerated. Should Virginians ever deem it necessary, those rights would revert to the state. This understanding, and assurances that a bill of rights was forthcoming, secured approval.[36]

Three days later word reached Richmond that on June 21, 1788 New Hampshire had been the ninth state to ratify, giving birth to America's Second Republic.

The Constitution had emerged from the convention a product of compromise not consensus, acceded to by states which were themselves unsure about what manner of "more perfect Union" they were creating. Once ratified, opponents of the Constitution said little more. Still, John Taylor of Caroline could not shake feelings of distrust. He hoped that eventually amendments might permanently trim federal power. Until that could happen Taylor advocated holding the line by the most conservative interpretation possible, a "strict construction" of every word in the document granting federal authority.[37]

He was to find it a losing battle. Soon after his disconcerting encounter with King and Ellsworth, Taylor resigned from the Senate, disgusted with what he called the self-serving partisanship of its members. He complained to Madison that his hair was "becoming white in the service" of Virginia. In 1796 John Adams of Massachusetts won the presidency and Federalists consolidated their hold on both houses of Congress and the judiciary. This led Taylor to begin pondering prospects for Southern independence. Thomas Jefferson attempted to talk him out of his secessionist feelings, arguing that Northeastern dominance and Federalist political ascendancy were afflictions to be endured but for a time. All that was needed, wrote Jefferson, was "a little patience and we shall see the reign of witches pass over." Jefferson conceded that "we are completely under the saddle of Massachusetts and Connecticut, and that they ride us very hard, cruelly insulting our feelings as well as exhausting our strength and subsistence." But this was "a temporary situation," to be rectified at the ballot box.

Taylor could not share Jefferson's optimism. "Checks and balances" between the three branches of the federal government were no guarantee of minority rights when a tyrannical majority controlled every department. The Constitution's safeguards were simply inadequate, there being no permanent security in the shifting winds of politics. The victory of one party over another Taylor likened to "a set of Indians gaming for shells." In such contests, "great art and talent are exhibited by the gamesters, and one side as well as the other, often win a game; but then the acquisition," he sadly observed, "is only a shell."[38]

III.

In 1797 President Adams dispatched Charles Cotesworth Pinckney, John Marshall and Elbridge Gerry to Paris to re-negotiate the old treaty with France, the alliance that had helped win American independence. France was warring with Great Britain and, as required by the 1778 treaty, insisted on American aid. Before talks could begin French Foreign Minister

Charles Talleyrand dispatched agents (individuals who would be publicly identified only as "X, Y and Z") to the American commissioners, calling for a loan of ten million dollars for the French government and a "gift" of one-quarter million dollars for Talleyrand himself. Americans were outraged when the attempted extortion became public, Pinckney demanding "millions for defense, but not one cent for tribute." The X Y Z affair set off an undeclared war between the United States and France on the high seas and an explosion of patriotism in America. Federalists like Senator Theodore Sedgwick immediately saw "a glorious opportunity to destroy faction" and demanded action against foreigners in America, chiefly French and Irish, and all who opposed the president's foreign policies.

In the summer of 1798 a Federalist Congress passed, and President Adams signed, a series of acts designed to strengthen the government's hand and silence domestic critics. The Naturalization Act extended the residence requirement for citizenship from five to fourteen years and two other laws dealing with the foreign-born expanded the president's power to deport enemy aliens in time of war and others he deemed "dangerous." The most controversial measure was the Sedition Act, passed on July 14. For a period of two years it was declared unlawful for anyone to "write, print, utter, or publish" anything "false, scandalous and malicious" against those in federal office. It was further declared seditious to bring Congress or the president "into contempt or disrepute" or to "excite against them...the hatred of the good people of the United States."[39] Less than seven years after the adoption of the Constitution's Bill of Rights a Federalist majority had cast aside the free speech protections of the First Amendment.

It was inevitable that outspoken Republican Thomas Cooper would be targeted by his Federalist foes. On October 26, 1799 the Reading, Pennsylvania *Weekly Advertiser* provoked Cooper, claiming that his and Priestly's opposition to John Adams stemmed from having been denied coveted government jobs. An indignant Cooper quickly broadcast a handbill defending himself and lashing out at the president. A few months later in a separate incident William Duane, Philadelphia newspaper editor and prominent Republican, criticized a bill before the Senate and published the text of the proposed legislation. The unfortunate Duane was ordered by Senate inquisitors to explain in person his "false, defamatory, scandalous and malicious" conduct. Cooper had been advising Duane on how to respond, though declining to legally represent him. Still, Cooper's prominence in the Duane affair irritated his enemies and reminded them of the offending handbill. Cooper was soon under general attack in the Federalist press and on April 9, 1800 was indicted under the Sedition Act.[40]

Ten days later his trial began. The handbill had specifically accused President Adams of misusing his authority by ordering a federal district judge in South Carolina to return a deserter to the British Navy. Cooper's charges, according to the prosecution, abounded with "foul and infamous falsehoods" against the president. An example must be made in this case, warned prosecutor William Rawle, because Cooper's criticism was not based on truth. "Error leads to discontent," he explained, "discontent to a fancied idea of oppression, and that to insurrection." Cooper, representing himself, pleaded not guilty, mocked the president's "newfangled doctrine of infallibility," and proceeded to ask for subpoenas of the chief executive, his secretary of state and a multitude of other officeholders. If Cooper had his way, complained one Federalist, Congress would be forced to adjourn in order to permit the vast number to testify. Cooper got nowhere with Judge Samuel Chase. Speaking to the jury on one occasion His Honor characterized the handbill as "the boldest attempt I have known to poison the minds of the people."[41]

Not surprisingly, Cooper was found guilty on May 1, sentenced to six months in prison, fined four hundred dollars and required to post a surety bond of two thousand dollars guaranteeing his "good behavior." Twenty-five would be indicted under the Sedition Act and Cooper became one of ten convicted. The man who had immigrated to America with his family in search of freedom of expression would learn while behind the bars of a federal prison that his wife Alice was dead. Federalists were delighted at his imprisonment, dismissing him as a demagogue deserving such punishment. But fellow Republicans hailed Cooper as a martyr and for the remainder of his life he was proud of having suffered in the cause of free speech.[42]

Visualizing how a declaration of war with France might once and for all solidify the Union, Alexander Hamilton broke with the more cautious Adams. Soon after leaving prison Cooper read reports of Hamilton's backbiting references to his president's "disgusting egotism," "distempered jealousy" and "the ungovernable indiscretion of Mr. Adams' temper." These words from an arch-Federalist were far stronger than any Cooper had dared to use. To publicize the glaring inconsistency in the hated law's enforcement Cooper traveled to New York to personally confront Hamilton with violating the Sedition Act. The former treasury secretary was out of town and managed to avoid his angry accuser.[43]

More difficult to ignore were the ringing protests that had been made in late 1798 and early 1799 by the legislatures of Kentucky and Virginia. Profoundly alarmed by Congress's curtailment of First Amendment rights, Madison drafted a resolution introduced in the Virginia legislature by John Taylor of Caroline. Taylor opened debate in the Virginia assembly by arguing that if the rights of aliens were abridged no one else could rest easy. Criticizing their leaders was "the first born of American rights" and any infringement of free speech must be dealt with immediately. Declaring the Alien and Sedition Acts to be unconstitutional, Virginia called for the cooperation of other states "in maintaining unimpaired the authorities, rights, and liberties reserved to the states respectively, or to the people." In Taylor's words, since "the Republicans have not fleets and armies; they appeal to public opinion for defense and support."[44] Faced with federal persecution, individuals were nearly helpless. But state governments, wrote Madison, could defend citizens' rights by the "interposition" of state authority on their behalf.

The resolution of the Kentucky legislature went even further in defining states' rights, declaring that whenever the federal government oversteps its bounds "its acts are unauthoritative, void and of no force." The states, as the parties to the federal compact, have the right to judge when violations of the Constitution have occurred as well as what ought to be done about them. Further encroachments on the rights of the people, "unless arrested on the threshold, may tend to drive these States into revolution and blood."[45]

Dominated by Federalist legislators, all of the Northern states denounced the Kentucky and Virginia resolutions. States may not determine the constitutionality of federal laws, replied New Hampshire — only the federal judiciary has that prerogative. For a state to stand in the way of federal authority might cause "civil discord," claimed Rhode Island, resulting in "many evil and fatal consequences." Vermont, having entered the Union as the fourteenth state after years as an independent republic, ventured the opinion that, "The people of the United States formed the federal constitution, and not the states." Madison expressed astonishment at such reasoning, instructing Northern Federalists that the very term "states" meant "the people composing those political societies in their highest sovereign capacity." Kentucky legislators answered their critics by passing another resolution. In it they declared that to allow the federal government to determine the extent of its own powers, through the federal judiciary or elsewhere, would lead to "despotism." Should federal authorities trample on the Constitution, the "rightful remedy" was "nullification" of the offending act by state intervention.[46]

Not until 1832 did it come to light that Thomas Jefferson had authored the Kentucky resolutions, the language of his original draft even stronger than that of the final version. In a 1799 letter to Madison, Jefferson went so far as to speak of the Kentucky and Virginia resolutions as a defense of the ultimate power "to sever ourselves from...the Union...rather than give up the rights of self government."[47]

During these troubled years Jefferson was serving as vice president, chosen in 1796 under the old rule that the position go to the candidate receiving the second highest number of electoral college votes. In 1800 he again challenged Adams for the presidency. This time Republicans were thoroughly aroused by the incumbent party's excesses, and Federalists were themselves divided. Jefferson won in a landslide, Republicans capturing control of both houses of Congress by large majorities. Only the judicial branch remained firmly in Federalist hands. Even after his defeat Adams nominated Federalist John Marshall to be chief justice of the Supreme Court and a lame duck Senate quickly confirmed the lifetime appointment. The routed Federalists, Jefferson wrote privately, "have retired into the judiciary as a stronghold." There, "preserved and fed from the treasury," he predicted their continued warfare against republicanism.[48]

On the morning of March 4, 1801 President-elect Jefferson walked from his Washington boardinghouse to the newly-constructed capitol, there to be sworn-in as America's third chief executive. In the final hours of his term Adams signed a stack of last-minute judgeship appointments, then hastened to Massachusetts without bothering to attend his successor's inauguration. For his part, Jefferson was willing to forget the past and forego vindictiveness. "We are all Republicans, we are all Federalists," said the new president in an inaugural address delivered in the Senate chamber. It was an "error of opinion," declared Jefferson, to advocate either an end to republican government or secession to save it. All that America needed now was "a wise and frugal Government," that encouraged agriculture and commerce, avoided "entangling alliances" and left the people as much freedom as possible. One "essential principle" that he promised would guide his administration was "support of the State governments in all of their rights, as the most competent administrations for our domestic concerns and the surest bulwarks against antirepublican tendencies..."[49]

The Naturalization Act was repealed in 1802, the Alien and Sedition Acts simply allowed to expire. The "reign of witches" was over, but John Taylor took little satisfaction in the Federalists' downfall. He feared the return of tyranny in the name of "majority rule." Had the offending laws been successfully nullified by state action, a more permanent "balance" might have been established between the federal and state governments. "There are no rights where there are no remedies," Taylor would write later, "or where the remedies depend upon the will of the aggressor."[50]

IV.

Members of the Charlotte County, Virginia grand jury came bounding down the courthouse steps while others climbed from the windows. Quickly they ran to catch up with the throng that had gathered around a platform built near the local tavern. Patrick Henry was about to speak! On this late winter day in 1799 Henry was no longer the young firebrand who had challenged King George with his "liberty or death" speech. The legendary patriot of the Revolution was now nearing the end of his life and afflicted by poor health. But forever there would be magic in the name Patrick Henry. When word came that he was to appear local schools canceled classes and farmers from the surrounding countryside gathered up their children and brought them to town. They might never have another opportunity to see and hear the great Virginian.

Henry was campaigning for election to the Virginia Senate. The previous Christmas Eve the state legislature had passed their resolutions condemning the Alien and Sedition Acts, proposing interposition as a remedy, and all Virginians were taking sides in the controversy. Henry had undergone a change of heart since his career as an anti-Federalist, and now stood before the crowd as one favoring the Commonwealth's acceptance of federal authority. There would be no debating the candidate this day, but the Republican viewpoint would at least be heard. John Randolph, freshman member of the Sixth Congress, was scheduled to say a few words.

"Is he going to speak against Old Pat?" one wide-eyed bystander asked. "Why he is nothing but a boy-he's got no beard!"

Some ventured the opinion that an older, more able man might better represent the Republican cause. "Never mind," replied a neighbor and friend of young Randolph, "he can take care of himself."

Slowly, Henry rose to speak. He began by expressing alarm at Virginia's immoderate protest of the Alien and Sedition Acts. Should the state actually put herself in opposition to federal authority civil war could result. He asked the people to picture George Washington at the head of a great army marching into Virginia charged with enforcing the law of the land. "Where is the citizen of America who will dare to lift his hand against the father of his country?"

From the rear of the crowd the town drunk began waving an arm as if to volunteer, but was quickly shamed for his insolence.

Henry reminded his audience that he had opposed Virginia's ratification of the Constitution. But the decision had been made. Now it was the duty of Virginians to obey the laws of the United States. Of course Americans could rise up in revolt should there be some actual infringement of their rights. But other avenues of redress were still available. To shatter the Union now would be to bid good-bye forever to freedom in a world ruled by monarchical tyranny.

As he finished Henry was engulfed by the weeping, applauding, worshipping crowd. Randolph himself stood for a time with tears in his eyes, as if overcome by emotion. He began his reply with an apology for rising in opposition to "the venerable father," but explained that he had learned his first political lessons in Henry's school. The federal government, created by the states and strictly limited in power, must never be allowed to become "the sole judge of its own usurpations." Virginia, in such a case, would have traded the tyranny of Old England for that of New England.

"Your Constitution broken, your citizens dragged to prison for daring to exercise the freedom of speech...and still you are told to wait for *some infringement* of your rights! How long are we to wait? Till the chains are fastened upon us, and we can no longer help ourselves?"

Randolph refused to flee from the specter of General Washington leading a federal army against his native state. Should such an outrage against Virginia ever materialize, "I trust there will be found many a Brutus to avenge her wrongs." The crowd went away stunned by the young man's eloquence and audacity.[51]

Randolph had taken his seat in Congress when just twenty-five years old, the minimum stipulated in the Constitution. His appearance was so youthful that the clerk of the House asked Randolph if he was indeed old enough to serve. "Ask my constituents," he replied without a smile. From Roanoke, his Virginia estate, Randolph brought bird dogs with him to Washington. He loved to hunt in the District, north of the capitol, and it became a common occurrence for the congressman to arrive at the House of Representatives "booted and spurred," with one or two of his dogs. When the door opened the animals would rush out onto the floor of the House chamber, sniffing at the members and creating a general disturbance.[52]

John Randolph was a descendant of Pocahontas and John Rolfe. As a boy he played outdoors and liked to fish, but his first love was reading. There was a large closet in his home lined with musty volumes and there he would spend countless hours. By age ten he had read widely in history, knew Shakespeare as well as the Arabian Nights and Don Quixote. Educated first at home, Randolph attended the College of William and Mary, the College of New Jersey (now Princeton) and later Columbia College in New York City. While in New York he attended George Washington's first inauguration and sat in on sessions of the First Congress.[53]

Randolph seemed always in poor health, a state that accentuated his eccentricities and provided no end of amusing stories. On one occasion, after suffering for days with fever, two doctors put their heads together and prescribed for him half a glass of Madiera. "Half a drop of rainwater would have been as efficient," grumbled Randolph. In the early hours of the morning he became delirious. Even then, he recounted later, "I had method in my madness; for they tell me I ordered Juba to load my gun and to shoot the first 'doctor' that should enter the room...'"

Once he fell gravely ill while in Philadelphia and was visited by a Quaker physician. "How long have you been sick, Mr. Randolph?"

"Don't ask me that question," replied the sufferer, "I have been sick all my life."

The doctor persisted. "There are idiosyncrasies in many constitutions. I wish to ascertain what is peculiar about you."

"I have been an idiosyncrasy all my life," confessed Randolph.[54]

Behind his peculiarities there burned in the heart of John Randolph of Roanoke a passion for liberty. "Love of peace, hatred of offensive war, jealousy of the state governments toward the general government," were touchstones of his political faith. He went on to profess "a dread of standing armies; a loathing of public debt, taxes and excises; tenderness for the liberty of the citizen; jealousy, Argus-eyed jealousy of the patronage of the President." Overeager lawmakers he likened to inexperienced young doctors, prone to prescribe the drug of governmental intervention in an attempt to cure society's ills. During one congressional campaign Randolph's opponent went perhaps a little too far in elaborating what he would do if elected. "He is in the land of promise," laughed Randolph, "which always flows with milk and honey."[55]

Randolph never quite trusted the Constitution's ability to guarantee liberty, and he found repugnant the notion that there was something sacred about that political association called the United States. "It was always my opinion," he would write, "that Union was the *means* of securing the safety, liberty and welfare of the confederacy, and not in itself an end to which these should be sacrificed." Proponents of increased federal spending he accused of twisting and stretching the plain meaning of the Constitution in order to find authority for their projects. The specific provision, for example, that Congress establish post offices and post roads meant simply that lawmakers were responsible for directing the mail, not for spending tax dollars on whatever "internal improvements" they thought expedient. During one such debate Randolph must have smiled at John Taylor's comment that, "happily the Constitution does not give to Congress a power to establish post canals." No matter. Randolph predicted that enthusiasts for internal improvements would "hook the power upon the first loop they find in the Constitution."[56]

Men of Randolph's and Taylor's fixed convictions were becoming anachronisms in the halls of Congress. Taylor, elected to fill a Senate vacancy, arrived on Capitol Hill in late 1822 and caused some to snicker at his coat, waistcoat, pantaloons and beaver hat, all from a generation past. Senator Taylor's out-of-style wardrobe, Randolph predicted, "will be rather nearer the fashion of the day than his principles."[57]

In 1819 came a ruling of the United States Supreme Court that was most troubling to "Old Republicans." Strict constructionists had for decades questioned the constitutionality of federal backing for the First Bank of the United States, but by 1816 even Republicans were voting to recharter the institution. Randolph claimed to discern among the bank's supporters a spirit "fatal to Republican principles; fatal to Republican virtues; a spirit to live by any means but those of honest industry." When the state of Maryland attempted to tax the Baltimore branch of the Bank of the United States, an institution competing with state-chartered banks, cashier McCulloch refused to pay and the state brought action to collect. The case made its way to the Supreme Court where Chief Justice John Marshall ruled against Maryland and went on to broadly define federal supremacy. Congress had the power to charter the bank because the act was "necessary and proper" to execute powers expressed in the Constitution. "Let the end be legitimate," wrote Marshall, "let it be within the scope of the Constitution, and all means which are appropriate, which are plainly adapted to that end, which are not prohibited, but consist with the letter and spirit of the Constitution, are constitutional."

Marshall's loose construction of the Constitution, according to Taylor, left few if any meaningful restraints on federal power. Virtually any act might be declared "necessary and proper" by its backers. It is, after all, the Constitution that is supreme, not the federal government. Taylor went on to argue that constitutional supremacy served to emphasize that document's "limitations, divisions, and restrictions of power," making the supremacy clause itself a bulwark against governmental growth and consolidation.[58]

Should there be a collision between the states and federal government the Supreme Court could never properly serve as judge, since it is itself a branch of the central authority. "A and B are at law with each other," in Taylor's example. "A has six men employed by great salaries to do his business, whom he can accuse himself, try himself, condemn himself, and dismiss himself. He proposes to B these very men as arbitrators between them. There is not a B in the whole world who would not laugh at the proposal. Gentlemen lawyers, is there one of you who would advise a client to listen for a moment to it?"[59] Marshall had concluded that sovereignty must reside at the national level since the federal government derived its authority from the people of America and exercised power "for their benefit." The people of America were indeed sovereign, ran the Republican counter-argument, but the United States government derived its powers from the people organized as states. And those states had not abdicated their sovereignty by delegating certain limited and specific powers to a general government.

The year after *McCulloch* v. *Maryland* Taylor published his views in *Construction Construed, and Constitutions Vindicated*. Thomas Jefferson made a rare public endorsement of the book, calling it "the most effectual retraction of our government to its original principles which has ever yet been sent by Heaven to our aid." The former president characterized the federal judiciary as a "subtle corps of sappers and miners constantly working under ground to undermine the foundations of our confederated fabric." Though Jefferson professed to having "little hope that the torrent of consolidation can be withstood, I should not be for giving up the ship without efforts to save her."[60]

In Randolph's view American freedom had most to lose from lawyers, politicians and those wearing judicial robes. "Sir, I never can forget, that in the great and good book to which I look for all truth and all wisdom, the Book of Kings succeeds the Book of Judges."[61]

V.

Like a sudden thunderstorm that shatters the stillness of a summer afternoon, Thomas Cooper's challenge to "calculate the value of the Union" had stunned his Columbia audience and left them gaping.

His foes were first to react. Alfred Bynum witnessed in person the Town Hall performance, jumping to his feet to declare Cooper's language "offensive and indelicate." The complete text of the speech was soon printed in the *Telescope* and copied by newspapers across the land. The Charleston *Courier* conceded the legitimacy of such protest gatherings, "But whenever such meetings…assault the permanency of the Union, it is time for all good men to give the alarm." Talk of breaking up the United States this editor branded as treason. "We believe it folly," he concluded, "and should it ever occur we doubt not it will end in ruin, irretrieveable ruin." A North Carolina newspaper professed shock that someone foreign-born would dare "preach up sedition and treason" against his adopted country. The New York *American* denounced "the presumption, the ingratitude, the intolerable audacity" behind Cooper's "traitorous suggestion." "He is a demon in human form," according to a writer in the *New York Courier and Enquirer*, "that would attempt to excite the South against the North, or the North against the South. He is an enemy in the land of Washington." Surely, hoped the Boston *Courier*, Cooper's language did not accurately reflect the feelings of South Carolina.[62]

The Charleston *Mercury* and Columbia *Telescope* were quick to come to Cooper's defense, though they stopped short of endorsing disunionism. Many of Cooper's supporters preferred to believe that he spoke in the "warmth of debate" and that his words should be taken in that context. "A Citizen," writing in the *Mercury*, expressed hope that the manufacturing interests would nevertheless heed Cooper's warning and "pause before they reach the edge of the precipice." Another letter defended Cooper against critics who act as if "the Union was formed for no purpose but to enrich those who violate its conditions."[63] While friends applauded his antitariff arguments, there was certainly no ground swell of support for the college president's incipient secessionism.

Cooper himself could not remain silent, responding first to those who discounted his words. "I will stand," said Cooper, "if they will give me leave, on my own ground, and deliberately re-adopt every syllable they complain of." The problem was misinterpretation of the document that had formed the Union. He had no objection to the Constitution "construed and enforced according to its plain meaning and its manifest original intention." He repudiated however, "the modern doctrine of liberal construction" that reduced the Constitution to "a piece of clay in the hands of the potter, and made to assume any shape that men in the seat of authority may find it their interest to direct." In a letter published in the Washington, D.C. *United States Telegraph* Cooper emphasized that he viewed secession as the last ditch defense against "systematic encroachments" on reserved rights and "perpetual perversions" of the Constitution. But clearly the time had come to question "whether the benefits we receive, are not more than counterbalanced by the evils we suffer."

His was a mind and spirit that permitted no compromise. The people had a responsibility to weigh the Union in the balance of their own interests and a right to find it wanting. "Now, if it be treason to believe and assert this, I am undoubtedly guilty, and am likely to continue so."[64]

Robert Barnwell Rhett

We aim not to be great but to be happy and free.

Robert Barnwell Rhett[1]

Prophet and Agitator
Robert Barnwell Rhett

Despite myriad protests and Thomas Cooper's fulminations, the Twentieth Congress of the United States in early 1828 passed what would become known as the "Tariff of Abominations." Average import duties were hiked to fifty percent, but revenue collected decreased as consumers simply stopped buying goods from abroad. Cooper's words were having an effect in South Carolina. Some urged the state's congressional delegation to walk out while others muttered darkly of breaking up the Union. Those in positions of responsibility seemed unable to decide what to do next, the political establishment fearful that extremist talk or precipitate action might jeopardize the re-election prospects of President Andrew Jackson and his running mate John C. Calhoun.[2]

Weeks passed. Then Robert Barnwell Rhett, young state legislator from Colleton District, issued a call for his constituents to meet him in the town of Walterboro on June 12. The sleepy little lowcountry village, shaded by ancient oaks wearing beards of Spanish moss, had never seen such excitement. In a public meeting two "addresses" were adopted by the citizens of Colleton. Both written by Rhett, the first was noncommittal, requesting only that Governor Taylor call the state legislature into session for the purpose of considering South Carolina's response to the tariff. The second address was a strident appeal for the people of the state to resist the tariff, even to the point of leaving the Union if necessary.

The level of duties imposed by the new act, argued strict constructionists, made a mockery of Congress's constitutional authority to regulate commerce. This tariff literally destroyed commerce. The South, ran the argument, now faced an implacable congressional coalition of Eastern protectionists and Westerners coveting federal money for their pet projects. The time had come for an ultimatum, concluded Rhett. If Congress refused to budge on the tariff issue South Carolina should permit no collection of revenue in the port of Charleston. If Northerners then failed to respond, rather than submit any further the state should leave the Union.

The Walterboro meeting and call to action created much initial excitement, though in the end Rhett was disappointed with the outcome. The Beaufort *Gazette*, edited by Rhett's brother-in-law John A. Stuart, supported the Colleton manifesto. But despite their activist reputations both the Charleston *Mercury* and the Columbia *Telescope* counseled moderation. The establishment stood firm. Governor Taylor refused to heed the call for a special legislative session and the presidential campaign went on without further embarrassment, Jackson and Calhoun sweeping to victory.[3]

His orchestration of the Colleton commotion was a fitting introduction of Robert Barnwell Rhett to a statewide audience. Two generations of South Carolinians would come to grin or grimace at the mention of his name.

That name was originally Smith. In 1837 he and his extended family changed their name to Rhett in order to honor a distinguished ancestor. Born in the coastal village of Beaufort, South Carolina in 1800, young Barnwell (as he was called) attended local schools where he was tutored by James L. Petigru, later a prominent attorney and unionist leader. At age nineteen Barnwell tackled the study of law in the offices of Charleston attorney Thomas Grimke, launching his own career as a lawyer two years later at Coosawatchie in Beaufort District. Soon thereafter he moved to Walterboro and entered into partnership with cousin Robert W. Barnwell.

In 1827 Rhett married Elizabeth Burnet, only seventeen but possessed of a quiet spirit that did much to counterbalance his own high-strung personality. "His temperament was nervous and mercurial," remembered a daughter, "he was quick in movement and quick tempered, but entirely self-controlled." Within the circle of his family and close friends Rhett could relax and joke, his blue-gray eyes sparkling when he laughed. Adored by his Colleton constituents and those of like-mind politically, Rhett was held in high regard too by some of the most steadfast of South Carolina unionists. Petigru and Rhett consistently stood at opposite ends of the political spectrum, but remained warm friends. Greenville unionist Benjamin F. Perry declared Rhett's career to be marked by "firmness, dignity, courtesy, and the unflinching pursuit of right according to the conscientious convictions of his own mind." A devout Episcopalian, Rhett saw to it that his slaves were taught the fundamentals of the Christian faith. Over the years he would serve as an officer in the Charleston Bible Society, the Young Men's Temperance Society and a port city group devoted to spreading the gospel among seamen.[4]

Others thought Rhett possessed of much less attractive traits. In a letter to Calhoun, Francis Pickens warned that Rhett was "*entirely* selfish" and "looking solely to office." H. W. Conner, president of the Bank of Charleston, believed that "exceedingly selfish" political ambition drove the man. One of Rhett's sons later claimed his father never attempted to curry favor and was "well known only to few." Still, Conner's unflattering characterization was the impression shared by many. Rhett was "a rash and ultra man in politics," wrote the conservative banker, "frequently bent upon extreme and desperate courses, very excitable and unstable and intolerant and contemptuous of all about him, with neither tact or discretion..."[5]

Young Barnwell Rhett was first elected to the South Carolina House of Representatives in 1826, representing St. Bartholomew's Parish in Colleton District. Chosen to serve on the Ways and Means Committee, by 1830 he had become its powerful chairman.

Two incidents early in Rhett's legislative career illustrate a "take charge" personality. A former governor, an honorable man but careless of details, had withdrawn several thousand dollars from the state's contingency fund and two legislative sessions had come and gone with no one requiring an accounting for the money. Despite his youth and lack of seniority, Rhett took a leading role in the successful campaign to require the comptroller general to investigate the situation. On another occasion during his first term Rhett chaired an impeachment committee. Judge William D. James' dependence on alcohol made him such an embarrassment that many were demanding term limits for judges and easier removal from office. Rhett feared that this would jeopardize judicial independence, but favored aggressive application of the legislature's impeachment powers. The committee, chaired by Rhett, brought charges against Judge James that resulted in a trial and conviction.[6]

Constitutionally, South Carolina in antebellum times was truly a "legislative state." Composed of Senate and House of Representatives, the General Assembly elected the governor (little more than an agent of the legislature, serving only two years and lacking veto power), nearly all state officers, United States senators and even presidential electors. Substantial property qualifications existed for those who would be lawmakers, though suffrage was open to all adult white males who had resided in the state for two years. Reapportionment of the legislature lagged far behind the reality of a shifting population, reserving a disproportionate number of seats for lowcountry planters. There were no political parties in South Carolina's General Assembly during the 1820s. Personalities were all-important, with loose coalitions the only political organization. As yet the question of state versus national supremacy decided no elections.[7]

From fiery champions of states' rights to ardent unionists, South Carolinians were overwhelming opposed to high tariffs and federally-funded internal improvements, essential elements of Henry Clay's

"American System." Southern agriculturalists complained that they were required to pay more than their fair share to support Northern industrial growth and road and canal building in the developing West. During the 1820s, as America struggled to recover from the deepest economic depression the country had suffered up to that time, South Carolina farmers and planters experienced a drastic drop in the price of cotton. In the midst of these hard times Congressman George McDuffie of Sumter made the sensational charge that out of every one hundred bales of cotton produced in the South, forty were in effect being transferred to the North by the Tariff of Abominations.[8] The congressman's calculations may have been less than scientific and perhaps exaggerated the true cost, but the "forty-bale theory" graphically pictured for South Carolinians the economic burden they believed that they were bearing.

A generation earlier it had been Northeasterners complaining of unequal burdens. During the Napoleonic Wars the Jefferson administration, by cutting off trade, had attempted to force Britain and France to respect the right of Americans to do business with both sides. But the prohibition served only to cripple New England merchants and ship owners. Angered by British arrogance, congressional "War Hawks" from the South and West, led by Calhoun and Clay, beat the drum for war. New England Federalists pleaded for peace and the preservation of trade.

When the United States declared war in June of 1812 few, especially in the South, had the foresight to comprehend the dangers that lay ahead or the courage to speak out. Offensive war, prophesied John Randolph of Roanoke, will "raze the constitution to its very foundations." For saying so in the face of patriotic fervor he was defeated at the next election. "The only certain consequence of war," worried John Taylor of Caroline, "except when it is undertaken for the purpose of repelling invasion, is that whichever side gains the victory, the people on both sides are vanquished."[9]

After a series of American defeats, including the burning of the United States Capitol and White House, the conflict would end in military stalemate. During the war a British blockade devastated New England's shipping and fishing industries. In the midst of hostilities delegates from five New England states met in Hartford, capital of Connecticut, to protest the war and what it was doing to the economic welfare of their people. What emerged were a series of resolutions that made it clear New England considered the South their rival within the Union. Representation in Congress should be based only on free inhabitants, they insisted, drastically reducing the number of Southern congressmen. There should be no new states admitted without a two-thirds vote of Congress, preserving the power of New England in the Senate. No president should succeed another from the same state, curtailing Virginia's domination of that office. Because the meetings were closed and members sworn to secrecy, rumors began to fly that the Hartford Convention contemplated secession. "Our Constitution is an affair of compromise between the States," pleaded John Randolph to a Hartford delegate. Any dispute between the sections over influence he hoped would be settled by "amicable discussion," not by "dissolving the confederacy."[10]

Sectional distrust was inflamed by the War of 1812. Another product of the conflict was the principle of protectionism. During the colonial period import duties ranged between one and five percent. After independence tariffs were the government's chief source of revenue, averaging eight and one-half percent. But in the aftermath of the War of 1812 many became convinced that America needed her own factories should war come again and the seas be controlled by enemy fleets. Most South Carolinians supported the protective features of the tariff of 1816 as necessary for national defense, a surrender of principle they would come to regret in decades to come. Randolph characteristically declined to jump aboard the bandwagon, rejecting patriotic appeals for protection of infant industries. As far as he was concerned, any tariff for other than revenue was simply a scheme by manufacturing interests to shamelessly exploit those engaged in agriculture. "We are the eel that is being flayed," he protested, "while the cookmaid pets us on the head and cries with the clown in *King Lear*, 'Down wantons, down.'" The "abracadabra of the constitution" worked no magic in securing Southern rights, declared Randolph, when "under the power to regulate trade, you draw the last drop of blood from our veins."[11]

On a voyage to Europe aboard the *Amity* in March 1822 a fellow passenger noticed Randolph going through a large box filled with books, all with worn covers. Questioned, Randolph explained that he was having them rebound in England.

"Bound in England!" exclaimed the amused gentleman. "Why did you not send them to New York or Boston, where you can get them done cheaper?"

"What sir," shot back Randolph, "patronize some of our Yankee taskmasters; those patriotic gentry, who have caused such a heavy duty to be imposed upon foreign books? Never, sir, never; I will neither wear what they make, nor eat what they raise, so long as my tobacco crop will enable me to get supplies from *old* England; and I shall employ John Bull to bind my books, until the time arrives when they can be properly done *South of Mason and Dixon's Line*!"[12]

II.

John Caldwell Calhoun as congressman, war secretary and seventh vice president of the United States had never been labeled a "sectionalist." Now, in the furor over the tariff, Calhoun's love for the Union led him to seek an outlet for the frustration and resentment building in his native South Carolina. If the Union was to be saved there must be some way, consistent with the Constitution, to resist federal usurpation. If not, South Carolina might very well be headed toward secession.

The Founding Fathers, reasoned Calhoun, had made inadequate provision to deal with competition between North and South. The sections, he noted, "so strongly distinguished by their institutions, geographical character, production and pursuits" were locked in a rivalry that threatened to bring down the very edifice of constitutional Union. Calhoun struggled with the problem, hopeful for the future yet haunted by fears. There must be some mechanism for guaranteeing minority rights within the Union, some way for the South to survive and prosper without resorting to secession.

In *The South Carolina Exposition and Protest* Calhoun argued that both union and liberty might be preserved as states sought redress through what he termed nullification. The people of the states, after all, had created the federal government. Should that government overstep its constitutional bounds the sovereign states were the logical bulwark to protect American liberty. If nullification seemed a desperate measure, one that perhaps created as many problems as it attempted to solve, Calhoun could only reply that it was simply necessary.[13]

Nothing short of a constitutional amendment, claimed proponents, could overrule a state once it acted to nullify a federal law. Critics countered that if three-fourths of the states, the majority required for amendment, was the final arbiter of constitutionality then a national sovereignty had in effect been created. Not so, replied advocates of state sovereignty. An overruled state merely by remaining in the Union gave its implied consent to an amended Constitution. Secession always remained the final option.

Calhoun and others felt the sting of criticism for a supposed inconsistency in their shift from "nationalism" to "sectionalism." Quite the contrary was true according to Henry L. Pinckney, founder of the Charleston *Mercury*. "[W]e have only changed," he explained, "from being friendly to a system which we once imagined would be *national*, to the opponents of a system which we are now convinced is *sectional* and *corrupt*."[14]

Nullifiers received mixed signals from outside the state. President Andrew Jackson, born in 1767 on the South Carolina-North Carolina frontier, proclaimed his "respect for state rights and the maintenance of state sovereignty." Nullifiers were further encouraged when Old Hickory refused to enforce a decision of the Marshall Court when it ruled against Georgia in a case involving that state and the Cherokee nation. Yet James Madison, now nearing eighty, came to discard nullification as a remedy available to the states. Though he understood the South's feelings about the tariff, in his opinion those grievances were not yet "so iniquitous and intolerable as to justify civil war, or disunion."[15]

Not all South Carolinians were nullifiers. While Rhett, William C. Preston and James Hamilton led the fight for nullification in the state legislature, they were opposed by a conservative though equally determined faction under the direction of Hugh S. Legare and others. Unionists wanted the state to protest the tariff, to be sure, but to go no further. Nullifiers demanded action should an appeal fail—action that would be taken by a convention excercising the sovereignty of the people. A legislative committee of seven, Rhett included, composed a formal protest while back home in Colleton District the *Gazette*, under Stuart's editorship, kept nullification on the front burner. Colleton was fast becoming what one described as "the Faneuil Hall where the cradle of Southern sovereignty is constantly rocked."[16]

In December 1830 nullifiers in the General Assembly introduced a resolution providing for the calling of a sovereignty convention. Rhett, member of the newly-formed Committee on Federal Relations, took a prominent part in preparing the convention resolution. Careful to avoid the word "nullification," the convention would be charged with protecting the rights of the state while at the same time preserving the Union. Unionist legislators proposed adding a statement to the resolution specifically disavowing nullification. Nullifiers, Daniel Huger charged, were intentionally avoiding the word in an attempt to deceive the people.

Rhett was outraged. Eyes flashing, he strode up to Huger, pointed a finger at him and declared that he "despised the man who endeavored to scare the people with nullification."

These were fighting words, the kind that too often led to bloodshed. Many expected a duel. Yet after a few hours Rhett's anger cooled. He began to consider the possibility that Huger had a valid point. Perhaps it was true that he and fellow nullifiers were not being open enough. In a move that took some courage Rhett stood on the floor of the House and apologized to Huger for his "hasty animadversions," putting an end to the prospect of a duel. Though most lawmakers favored the convention resolution, it failed to gain the necessary two-thirds majority. For now there would be no convention.[17]

Huger's words had an unintended effect as nullifiers immediately became more bold. Across South Carolina "State Rights and Free Trade Associations" were organized. Stuart carried on the crusade as editor of Charleston's *State Rights and Free Trade Evening Post*, moving a few months later to the Port City's influential *Mercury*. Nullifiers soon demonstrated superiority in leadership, organization and an ability to reach the undecided with their message. For over a year, beginning in the summer of 1831, the struggle raged across the Palmetto State. At one point mobs of toughs battled in the cobblestone streets of Charleston, sailors joining the ranks of whichever side offered the most liquor. Unionists published a letter from Andrew Jackson appealing for South Carolinians to rally to the federal government. If nothing else, the letter forced many citizens to confront the question of their primary loyalty. In response, Rhett met again with his constituents in Walterboro and they fired off a resolution to the president.

For his information, allegiance to South Carolina was "natural" and permanent, declared the people of Colleton District. In contrast, loyalty to the Union was conditional and might in fact be terminated.[18]

In an Independence Day 1832 speech to his constituents, Rhett demanded more than words from the state's leaders. Nullification was the kind of "redress" needed to deal with the tariff, a form of resistance not inconsistent with the Constitution and Union. But he did not stop there. If unionists sought to discredit him with the epithet "revolutionary," he refused to run from the label. "What, sir, has the people ever gained, but by Revolution?...What sir, has Carolina ever obtained great or free, but by Revolution?...Revolution! Sir, it is the dearest and holiest word, to the brave and free..."

Benjamin Franklin Perry would never deny the American people's right to revolution nor could he turn his back on South Carolina, however much he opposed nullification. Editor of the *Greenville Mountaineer*, Perry went so far as to challenge a rival editor to a duel over words he thought "scurrilous and abusive," and killed the nullifier. Still, Perry's commitment to the Union was conditional, and illustrated a weakness in the ranks of South Carolina unionists. An incongruous collection of upcountry small farmers, Charleston merchants and lawyers, they were united only in their opposition to nullification. They differed on such essential questions as the constitutionality of the tariff and the right of state secession. As the campaign progressed, unionists seemed sluggish and their efforts grew sporadic.[19]

Rhett could only smile at the course of events. A special session of the General Assembly that met on October 22, 1832 quickly and overwhelmingly called for a convention. Election of delegates was held in less than three weeks and the convention convened in Columbia six days later. Candidates committed to nullification ran unopposed in the lowcountry and swept to victory nearly everywhere else. Upcountry unionists picked up a few seats, choosing to attend though hopelessly outnumbered.[20]

On November 24 "the people of the State of South Carolina in Convention assembled" declared "null, void and no law" the Tariff Acts of 1828 and 1832. Effective February 1, 1833 federal duties would no longer be collected within the state. Delay in the ordinance's enforcement was designed to give the United States Congress time to reconsider. A challenge to nullification was expected in the federal courts. But should Congress decide to use force against the Palmetto State that act would break the bond of union. The state's response to attempted coercion, declared the convention, would be immediate secession and the establishment of an independent republic. "There was something so heart-cheering and inspiring in the mode of ratification," reported one enthusiastic participant. "The seven patriots and war-worn soldiers of the revolution, going up to sign their names—the crowd around the table—the anxiety to affix their signature to an instrument, which, like the Declaration of Independence, was to endure forever − the joy beaming on the countenance of all, that the great work of reform was at last begun."[21]

"To count the cost," observed Miss Maria Pinckney, "has never been characteristic of Carolinians!" President Jackson beefed up the federal garrisons at Fort Moultrie and Castle Pinckney, strongholds guarding Charleston harbor. General Winfield Scott was put in charge of military preparations as Old Hickory forwarded five thousand muskets for the use of a unionist "private army" that Joel Poinsett was said to be raising. "We shall cross the mountains into...South Carolina," announced Jackson, "with a force, which joined by the Union men of that State, will be so overwhelming as to render resistance hopeless." The president threatened to immediately begin arresting nullification leaders on charges of treason. Calhoun, having resigned the vice presidency and returned to Washington as senator from South Carolina, was awakened late one night by a friend. Congressman Robert Letcher of Kentucky breathlessly told him that he had just come from the White House where Jackson talked of hanging Calhoun for treason. In an atmosphere such as this there seemed scant hope of compromise.[22]

The president's December 10, 1832 "Proclamation to the People of South Carolina" stated forcefully his view of federal supremacy. States joining the Union gave up many of the functions of sovereignty, convincing Jackson that a portion of sovereignty itself had therefore been irrevocably surrendered. The federal government had the inherent right to defend itself, according to Jackson, and that meant it must enforce federal law in the face of nullification. And it must fight rather than allow the secession of member states.

To Rhett the proclamation was outrageous. In his view Jackson's interpretation of the federal compact was a revision that reduced Americans to the level of Prussian peasants or the serfs of Russia. To make matters worse, Jackson sent Congress a "Force Bill" detailing his plan for collecting the tariff in South Carolina, legislation that authorized him to use the army and navy against such "insurgents" as failed to "disperse." Calhoun could only describe the Force Bill as a "virtual repeal of the Constitution." Duff Green, Senate printer and Calhoun partisan, dutifully published the bill when it was reported out of committee, but made his own feelings clear by bordering the columns in black.[23]

A series of debates were held in the Senate, climaxing in a Calhoun exchange with Daniel Webster. The Massachusetts Senator's soaring nationalistic oratory was met by the cold, hard logic of his opponent. John Randolph of Roanoke came, now a private citizen but anxious to support Calhoun and the cause of states' rights. Randolph was in declining health, only recently returned from frigid St. Petersburg where he served as American ambassador to Russia. In the Senate gallery the diminutive Randolph had difficulty getting a good view of the proceedings. "Take away that

hat," he pleaded to another spectator, "I want to see Webster die, muscle by muscle."

Predictably, Senate debate changed few minds on either side. When time came for a vote the outcome was so inevitable that Southern senators staged a walkout. Only Virginia's John Tyler stayed behind, to cast his lone vote against the Force Bill.[24]

Southerners had no love for the tariff and only scorn for Jackson's threats. But neither did many support this thing called nullification. The legislatures of Alabama, Georgia and Mississippi denounced South Carolina's action. Virginia too went on record in opposition to nullification, but at the same time condemned the president's proclamation and reaffirmed the right of state secession.[25]

Down in South Carolina preparations went forward to resist a federal invasion. The General Assembly had already voted to spend $400,000 for military purposes and authorized the governor to call out the militia, enroll volunteers and even institute a draft if needed. On the day after Christmas Governor Robert Young Hayne asked for volunteers and 25,000 men stepped forward. What they lacked in training and equipment they made up for in enthusiasm. Across the state the blue-uniformed troops of the South Carolina Militia drilled, cheered by civilians defiantly wearing blue cockades. Grave officers pored over maps as they planned to besiege Fort Moultrie and reduce Castle Pinckney with cannon fire. Governor Hayne, reasoning that a premature concentration of state troops might provoke hostilities, ordered his volunteers to continue training near home. Each district would have one hundred "mounted minutemen" on stand-by, a total of two thousand eight hundred soldiers prepared to fly immediately to any threatened point in the state. The governor spoke in solemn tones of "those rights and liberties, which we are bound, by every tie divine and human, to transmit unimpaired to our posterity." Members of the General Assembly wept openly as he confessed love and loyalty to the land of his birth, declaring that come what may, "we will STAND OR FALL WITH CAROLINA."[26]

Henry Clay was thoroughly alarmed. Determined to do what he could to head off an outbreak of war, he held secret meetings with Calhoun. South Carolina authorities, hoping for some palatable compromise, let pass their self-imposed February first deadline. Eleven days later Clay introduced a compromise tariff bill that Calhoun could support. Duties would be substantially reduced, gradually rolled back over a period of nine years. Though the principle of protectionism remained, New England manufacturing interests screamed in protest at the compromise. Most Americans breathed a sigh of relief. The new tariff quickly passed both houses of Congress and all eyes turned to South Carolina for their response.

Calhoun felt that nullification had accomplished all that it could. Little South Carolina had declared a law of the United States "null and void," and that law had been replaced. The delegates in Columbia must understand that a victory had indeed been wrestled from their foes. To go further, to demand a total end of protectionism, would jeopardize all that had been won. Calhoun boarded the next mail coach headed south, and after eight miserable days and nights on the road reached the South Carolina capital. He immediately went before the convention, pleading for acceptance of the compromise.

His words had their effect. A few, such as Robert Turnbull and Thomas Cooper, wanted to forge ahead in a battle of wills with Andrew Jackson. Most, including Rhett, came over to Calhoun's way of thinking. Rhett had been elected to the convention but was unable to attend the first meeting due to illness. Now in the March session he considered the alternatives, pondered South Carolina's position, listened to Calhoun and reluctantly went along with the compromise.

The fact that it *was* a compromise, and not the settlement he yearned for, made his "aye" vote a bitter anticlimax. Still brooding, Rhett was in no mood for the committee report that pronounced the outcome of nullification a "cause for congratulation and triumph." He moved that the word "triumph" be deleted. The report went on to declare South Carolina's "ardent attachment to the Union." Rhett leaped to his feet, demanding there be no blatant hypocrisy. "I ask the gentlemen upon this floor whether they can lay their hands upon their hearts, and say, that they are 'ardently attached to the Union...'" If they were truly honest with themselves, he asked, would they not consider the formation of a Southern confederacy a far happier ending? The principle of protectionism remained. Coercion of the states loomed more real than ever. South Carolinians must understand that nothing had been permanently resolved, that the real fight still lay ahead.[27]

This was not what the convention wanted to hear. Members chose instead to make one final gesture of defiance. Judge William Harper proposed that after revoking South Carolina's nullification of the tariff, the convention should show its contempt for the threat of federal coercion by nullifying the Force Act. Radicals considered this gesture laughable. "I should like to see you nullify the army provisions of that bill," said a sneering McDuffie. It would take more than a piece of parchment, growled the congressman, to render "null and void" the army and navy of the United States.[28] Quixotic though it was, nullification of the Force Act was the convention's parting shot at Andrew Jackson.

Despite Rhett's pessimistic outlook, nullification had shaken the "American System" to its foundations. One small state had forced the federal government to substantially reduce its tariff. "Congress," commented Alexis de Tocqueville, "which had been deaf to the complaints of its suppliant subjects, listened to them when they had arms in their hands." Still, passage of the Force Act had established a precedent for future coercion of states should the federal government ever deem that necessary. The

Palmetto State's leaders, responding to Rhett's demand that "South Carolina must be an armed camp," worked to bolster the militia. The state, in
Rhett's view, must never speak but from a position of strength.[29]

Part of that strength would come from a people less divided. After
years of confrontation, nullifiers set about wooing and conciliating the
unionist minority, peacemaking that would pay dividends in the decades
to come. Thomas Cooper pinned his hopes on "the good sense and noble
bearing of this little State." When he died in 1839 there was carved on his
cemetery monument the revealing postscript that the memorial was
"ERECTED BY A PORTION OF HIS FELLOW CITIZENS." Yet the "School-
master of States' Rights" had done his job well. South Carolinians in increasing numbers came to embrace his political views, the new generation
ever more willing to consider a future for the state outside of the Union.

"I yield slowly and reluctantly to the conviction that our constitution
cannot last," confessed John Marshall to Justice Joseph Story. "The union
has been prolonged thus far by miracles. I fear they cannot continue."[30]

III.

In the aftermath of nullification Rhett backed away from revolutionary brinksmanship, withdrawing to a place of study and introspection. He
mastered the reading of French, enjoyed poetry, studied history and delved
into Calhoun's political theories and constitutional remedies. Rhett's law
practice and a newly-acquired plantation claimed much of his attention.
Yet he did not entirely desert the political arena, serving for a time as South
Carolina's attorney general.

He would re-enter the fray reluctantly. In 1836 William J. Grayson,
forty-seven-year-old congressman from Beaufort, South Carolina, chose to
retire. Grayson wrote to Rhett, urging him to toss his hat in the ring, and
with little enthusiasm Rhett agreed to make the attempt. After securing
support from some of the district's most influential leaders, Rhett abandoned the campaign due to illness and perhaps apathy. While in the more
healthful climate of eastern Tennessee word came that Grayson had re-
entered the race. Not until after election day did Rhett return home, amazed
that he had been elected to the United States House of Representatives
without troubling to run for the seat.[31]

The new congressman defended nullification in his maiden speech,
then spurned Jackson's Democrats to sit with the Whigs. He looked to
Calhoun for leadership, learned parliamentary procedure and strived to
avoid personal clashes with his colleagues. Soon after taking his seat he
and other Southerners were angered by an abolitionist's proposal that slavery be outlawed in the District of Columbia. Southerners held that the
federal government had not been created to take sides for or against slavery, an institution always managed by the states. The Constitution ought
to be amended, said Rhett, adding language to it that would explicitly and

forever deny congressional authority over slavery. A Southern convention should convene to demand either this kind of permanent security or a peaceful dissolution of the Union. Much to Rhett's disgust, the majority of Southern congressmen were satisfied to state their objections, then return to business as usual. It was a defeat he would not forget.

By 1840 Rhett was back in the Democratic camp, placing his faith in that party's ability to rightly interpret the Constitution and thus protect Southern rights and interests. When the tariff was renewed in 1842, at near 1832 levels, he was bitterly disappointed. He dreamed of Calhoun's election to the highest office in the land and encouraged the senator's presidential prospects with trips to other states and mending of fences at home. Along with Calhoun, Rhett moderated his long-standing opposition to federally-funded internal improvements. For years he had denied their constitutionality. As state legislator Rhett challenged South Carolina's congressmen to defeat all such appropriations, even if the money was to be spent in the Palmetto State. Now he thought that perhaps by backing down on this issue the South might make an accommodation with the West. Though Westerners stood to benefit from free trade, reasoned Rhett, they would continue to vote with the industrial Northeast if it meant government aid. Rhett's flirtation with logrolling was short-lived however, and he soon returned to the strict constructionism he felt most comfortable defending.[32] But the episode illustrated a mind in conflict. Should he place his faith in political parties and their leaders or in his own intuition? Could more be gained by accommodation or by breaking the rules?

When Congress adjourned in June 1844 Rhett stayed behind in Washington to prepare an address to his constituents. Published ten days later in the *Mercury*, it called for a new state convention to tackle the tariff. Once again excitement was in the air. Rhett was welcomed home the last day in July with a dinner in his honor in Bluffton, South Carolina. It was a temperance affair naturally, as the congressman was a "teetotaler," but Rhett needed no stimulant to deliver an emotional exhortation calling for renewed resistance to the tariff. Other dinners and more speeches followed. The *Mercury* fired a broadside in support and the "Bluffton Movement" was under way.

Rhett was not trying to stage a mutiny against Calhoun, a man "whose shoe-latchets as a statesman I am unworthy to loose," but to prod the senator and South Carolina into a more aggressive stance. The time had come, said Rhett, for a state convention to issue an ultimatum demanding that the Union return to what it had been when the Constitution was ratified — a place where South Carolina felt secure. Failing that, the state should withdraw. "I hold the Constitution in politics as I do the Bible in religion," stated Rhett. "My object is not to destroy the Union, but to maintain the Constitution, and the Union too, as the Constitution has made it." The time had come when only "strong measures" — actions that put the Union itself in danger — might save it.

The "Bluffton Boys" preached Rhett's message of threatened secession throughout the districts of Beaufort, Barnwell, Colleton and Orangeburg. A few state leaders, such as George McDuffie and James Hammond, joined the chorus calling for a convention. Even conservative Langdon Cheeves asked for united action by the Southern states up to and including secession. Such talk could only encourage Rhett, but experience in Congress had shown him that Southern cooperation was "next to impossible." If one state would lead the way—should South Carolina provoke the federal government into attempting to use force—then all the South would surely unite. "In our revolution, no assemblage of the colonies was held until the tea was thrown overboard in Boston Harbor," said Rhett. "[A]nd so it can be again. All we want, is that the tea shall be thrown overboard—that the issue be made."

Whigs certainly made an issue of Rhett's words, attempting to embarrass the Democrats in an election year, and the Bluffton excitement began to wind down. Calhoun called on Democrats to close ranks and the party ended up carrying the state. Rhett was himself re-elected without opposition, but a few expressed displeasure with him by casting blank ballots. If nothing else the failed Bluffton Movement had, in Joel Poinsett's words, "trained to the work of agitation" fresh troops for the coming struggle.[33]

The congressional tariff legislation that finally did emerge, the Walker Tariff of 1846, was far from the free-trade goal Rhett desired. Still, it imposed duties less burdensome than those of most European countries and Rhett supported it as a step in the right direction.

Protectionism remained Rhett's primary grievance, but to many other Southerners antislavery agitation was fast becoming their greatest cause for alarm. As early as 1838 Thomas Cooper prophesied that slavery would, "ultimately, like Aaron's rod, swallow up" all other sectional disputes.[34] Even as they drove a wedge between North and South, abolitionist attacks predictably worked to unite Southerners in a determination to resist outside interference.

As South Carolina approached mid-century unionism became increasingly a minority view. Unconditional loyalty to the federal government was nearly extinct. The majority sought redress and security through cooperation among the Southern states. South Carolina might take the lead, said these cooperationists, just so long as she was not left isolated and vulnerable. Rhett and others, concluding that cooperation was hopeless, favored unilateral action. In September 1848 Rhett told a Charleston audience that Southern cooperation would come when South Carolina had taken radical measures, not before. "She can force every State in the Union to take sides, for or against her. She can compel the alternative—that the rights of the South be respected, or the Union be dissolved."[35] But separate state action must come first.

Near death and deeply troubled over the future of his country and the South, Calhoun predicted that "within twelve years" the Union would be dissolved. "The probability is, that it will explode in a presidential election."

He died in Washington City on the last day of March 1850. Even amid the mourning period, down in South Carolina maneuvering began for his vacant post in the Senate. Governor Whitemarsh Seabrook made interim appointments, but the two leading candidates for election by the General Assembly were James Hammond and Barnwell Rhett. With all his heart Rhett wanted the job. Perhaps he saw himself wearing the mantle of the irreplaceable Calhoun. He led the voting from the first, won on the legislature's fourth ballot and took his seat January 6, 1851.[36]

Senator Rhett was a delegate to the Nashville Convention in June, one more futile effort to secure cooperation among Southerners for secession. Though he took no prominent part on the floor, he did write the convention's "Address," and came away more convinced than ever that South Carolina must act alone. The summer before, speaking in Charleston, Rhett suggested that "to maintain the Constitution, we must dissolve the Union, to afford the only hope of restoration." The initial response to his words seemed encouraging. He clarified himself a little later to a Macon, Georgia audience, calling for at least one state to leave the Union temporarily. Within two years of secession, he predicted, the North would be more than willing to make whatever concessions were necessary to reconstruct a Union friendly toward Southern rights. If not, every Southern state would then depart to form a great new confederacy, perhaps joined by California and the territories of Utah and the Southwest. In either case, South Carolina should lead the way.[37]

To that end Rhett had met with state legislators in Columbia in late November 1850, lobbying for a secession convention. Lacking the two-thirds majority needed to have their way, radicals were still able to schedule elections to a convention that would act on the proposals of a yet-to-meet Southern Congress. Rhett himself would not be a candidate for election to the convention, perhaps because he now resided in Charleston and that city was beginning to feel apprehension over what effect independence might have on business. Secessionists were becoming apathetic. A conservative reaction was in fact settling in all across South Carolina as people began to fear isolation from the rest of the South. Greenville unionist Benjamin Perry founded the *Southern Patriot* to rally upcountry opposition to disunionism. With the tide turning against his cause, Rhett and his allies decided to stage one more counterattack.[38]

IV.

Nearer to the appointed meeting time gentlemen would throng the steps that led up to the tall wooden doors, talking excitedly, laughing and greeting friends. Now those arriving early could linger outside in the cool air. Here at the portico of Hibernian Hall was a fine vantage point from which to experience an April evening in Charleston. Traffic in front of the hall was sparser at twilight, the bustle of Meeting Street kept at bay by a high fence fashioned of iron, its central gate crowned with the pleasant outline of an Irish harp. As the roofs and spires of the old city disappeared in the advancing darkness, from a thousand raised windows came the glow of lamplight, the sounds of soft voices and a muted rattle of china and silver. At the Hibernian Society's Greek temple the flickering street lamps projected darting shadows onto the six massive Ionic columns. Silent and dark across the street reposed the fireproof Records Building. On a sight just a few steps away the forward-looking directors of the newly-chartered South Carolina Institute had plans to erect an exhibition hall. Off to the right, where Meeting Street joined Broad, the soaring steeple of Saint Michael's Church dominated the sky. On the hour tolled her eight bells, as they had since before the Revolution, answered by the chimes of Saint Phillip's on Church Street, next to the resting place of Calhoun.

Members of the Hibernian Society, a long-established fraternal and benevolent order, had raised their handsome building just a decade earlier. Charlestonians claiming Irish descent were careful to avoid all sectarianism, leadership of the society alternating between a Protestant and a Roman Catholic. Besides Saint Patrick's Day feasts and the annual ball of the Saint Cecilia Society, the facility was available for a variety of other events. The Southern Rights Association had booked the hall for their scheduled meeting of April 7, 1851. The *Mercury*, determined to dispel apathy and keep up the drumbeat for secession, heavily promoted the gathering. Senator Rhett would speak to the faithful. More important was the impact his words might have on the wavering majority outside, particularly Charlestonians, who would read the speech and hear his arguments repeated in the days and weeks to come.

The *Mercury*'s reporter surveyed the assembled multitude and decided that the crowd was "large and enthusiastic." Rhett acknowledged their welcome and began his remarks by pronouncing dead all hope of cooperation. "Our sister Southern States decline our solicitation to meet us in counsel." Paralyzed by this spirit of submission, any Southern Congress that did meet would be worse than useless. The choice had become "submission, or secession by South Carolina alone." With the failure of their strategy Rhett now called on cooperationists to back unilateral independence for South Carolina.

What would independence bring? According to the senator, a Carolina Republic would immediately establish free trade with the Southern states remaining in the Union. The imports of Northern and Western states of the United States, as well as the imports of other foreign countries, would be subject to a modest revenue duty of ten percent. Since the average level of the current tariff was thirty percent, imports would become twenty percent cheaper for the state's consumers. Northern merchants "look upon the secession of South Carolina from the Union with alarm and terror," said Rhett. "We must gain what they lose," free trade inevitably funneling business to the port of Charleston.

What if the president resorted to a blockade? "Blockade is war," answered Rhett, and "if any one supposes that war in any form can be made on South Carolina without fighting, he is not worth reasoning with." Should federal authorities fight to force the state back into the Union, the entire South would instantly rally to her aid. "The right of secession is the right of all. Surrender it, and the States are no longer sovereignties." Should coercion be attempted, "a Southern Confederacy is as sure to come as the succeeding year." Some of the smaller Northern states would not jeopardize their own sovereignty by waging war on the South, Rhett predicted, and many Northern Democrats would find it impossible to deny the people of South Carolina their right to self-determination. "My friends," the senator prophesied, "I am satisfied that if South Carolina thinks proper to go out of the Union, she will go out without a single hostile gun being fired, or a single tombstone being erected to tell a tale of martyrdom. On expressing such conviction to a distinguished officer of our State, immediately on my return from Washington, he exclaimed – 'No fighting, well, that is the worst news I have heard for a long time! How, in the name of heaven, are we to get the Southern Confederacy?' I answered – 'By just Government and a superior liberty.'"

After South Carolina's departure would come a chorus of appeals and proposed concessions designed to prevent further defections. Once secession was accomplished however, Rhett insisted that there be no reconstruction without "entire redress for the past and security for the future." From the Northern states there would have to be ironclad guarantees that no federal expenditures be made for objects not expressly authorized by the Constitution. Eschewing protectionism, modest duties could be imposed for revenue only. Toward slavery Congress must remain scrupulously neutral, as the Constitution intended. "Disunion, and disunion forever, or all our rights," exclaimed Rhett, "should be our fixed and unalterable determination." Regarding internal improvements, the tariff and slavery South Carolina had but one demand: "Let us alone."

To the objection that the independence of South Carolina would bring added military, naval and diplomatic expense, Rhett's response was blunt. "It is not for freemen to count the cost of Free Government." In any case, within five years after South Carolina's secession he predicted that either the Union would be reconstructed on terms of Southern "safety, liberty, and equality," or the state would be part of a new confederacy.

"I have been battling in this cause for twenty-five years," concluded Rhett, "and have now but a few more years to give to your service. I long to see it settled. As a citizen of South Carolina, I demand that she make me free. Let her determine, now and forever the fate of her sons. My counsel is, secede from the Union of these United States...If I was about to draw my last breath I would exhort you to secede. And above all, my friends, let us be united in secession..."[39]

———————

The following month 431 Southern Rights Association delegates, representing forty local organizations from around the state, met in Charleston. Radicals were in firm control and demanded the secession of South Carolina by separate state action. Other Southern states remained silent and enthusiasm around South Carolina seemed lacking. No one expected a Southern Congress to meet, but all factions in the state now looked to October's election of delegates as a decisive test of strength. Conservatives — those who professed to favor a Southern confederacy, but only in eventual cooperation with other Southern states — now cooperated with unionists in order to defeat the radicals and stave off precipitate action by South Carolina. When the votes were counted Rhett's old congressional district was the only one to elect a majority of "separate state actionists." Elsewhere across the state cooperationists swept to victory by comfortable margins.

Rhett returned to Washington defeated and depressed. In a December 1851 speech he vehemently defended on the Senate floor the right of state secession. Out of step with his Southern colleagues — an embarrassment — he was ignored by most and even insulted by a few. Alabama Senator Jeremiah Clemons attempted to provoke a duel by calling him a traitor and a coward. Rhett's refusal to fight the Senator, based as it was on his Christian faith, brought a measure of sympathy and understanding. Some noted that Rhett seemed to be on better terms personally with the Senate's abolitionist members.

The South Carolina convention finally met in the spring of 1852, fractured and purposeless even before the first session was called to order. Though not a member, Rhett attended. Delegates eventually passed a resolution reaffirming secession as the state's right and eventual objective. Strong words, to be sure, but Rhett craved action.

Deeply discouraged at this policy of "absolute submission," Rhett sat down and composed a letter of resignation from the Senate. He no longer considered himself "a proper representative" of South Carolina's way of thinking. The resignation, springing from adherence to principle and a sense of honor, earned the respect of even his political enemies. Perry termed the act "noble and patriotic." Rhett returned home to "make way for those, who, with hearts less sad, and judgements more convinced, can better sustain her in the course she has determined to pursue."[40]

We are not revolutionists; we are resisting revolution. We are upholding the true doctrines of the Federal Constitution. We are conservative. Our success is the triumph of all that has been considered established in the past.

James Henley Thornwell[1]

Countering Lincoln's Revolution
James Henley Thornwell

James Henley Thornwell, sixth president of South Carolina College, walked across his quiet campus, relieved that the immediate danger had passed. "The prospect of disunion," he had confided to a friend, "is one which I cannot contemplate without absolute horror." Such a thing could not be accomplished peacefully, and "a war between the States of this confederacy would, in my opinion, be the bloodiest, most ferocious, and cruel, in the annals of history."

Thornwell had stood like an oak amid the howling secessionist storm that swept through the state. Conservative to the core, he saw the United States as an "apostle of civilization, liberty, and Christianity" and confidently assured his students that Americans "stand, indeed, in reference to free institutions and the progress of civilization, in the momentous capacity of the federal representatives of the human race." The secession of a single state might well precipitate a chain reaction, resulting in a multiplication of regional confederacies, blasting his expectations for a united America. Besides, it would be dangerous to make so revolutionary a move in the midst of an "age of tumults, agitation, and excitement, when socialism, communism, and a rabid mobocracy seem everywhere to be in the ascendant." In a real sense, the "liberty of the world is at stake."

Thornwell the evangelical Christian was certain he recognized God's hand of blessing on the United States. There was no other explanation for America's rise to greatness in but two generations. He was proud of the part his country was playing in world evangelism, and mindful too of an

James Henley Thornwell

Life and Letters of James Henley Thornwell

implicit warning. From America the church "stretches its missionary arm across the globe—we can not interrupt this divine task with civil strife." The chaos and upheaval of war could only cripple the work of reaching the lost with the gospel and invite God's wrath. "Our glory is departed—the spell is broken—whenever we become divided among ourselves." Christians must become promoters of peace and sectional reconciliation. "The interests of the Savior's kingdom are too intimately connected with the permanence and prosperity of this great confederacy, to allow any disciple to be a calm spectator of passing scenes."[2]

At the height of the secession agitation Thornwell had nearly thrown up his hands in despair at keeping South Carolina in the Union, resigning himself to "sharing her fortunes" as his state plunged into the unknown. Though some embraced secession as the ultimate security for slavery, Thornwell cautioned that the institution would be in greater danger from meddlesome Northern and British abolitionists should South Carolina come out from behind the shield of the Union. Those antislavery extremists were the root of the problem. He appealed to Christians in the North to help put down a movement "which aims alike at the destruction of the Government and the subversion of religion." If, in fact, abolitionist Northerners offended by Southern slavery "cannot, consistently with their convictions of duty, maintain the neutrality which the Federal Constitution requires; if they cannot, in other words, observe the conditions which they have voluntarily agreed to observe; they ought, in all frankness and candour, to withdraw from the contract, and openly proclaim that it is at an end with them." As they have no constitutional power to interfere with slavery in the South, "their consciences should not be pressed for not doing what they have no right to do."

For now Thornwell advised patience and watchfulness. "When we are driven to despair of the Republic," he counseled fellow Southerners, "and not till then, shall we be justified in withdrawing." He was willing to concede that secession might one day become a necessary evil, but only should the federal government become "hopelessly perverted" or "openly pledged to the extinction of slavery." In such a circumstance, but only then, "it will be our duty, as it is our right, to provide for ourselves."[3]

———

After the death of her husband Martha Thornwell had bravely faced the task of providing for her four children, including eight-year-old James. A devout Baptist, only her faith could carry her through the difficult years ahead. James' father had been a Marlboro District plantation overseer, described as "living always up to his means, and accumulating nothing." Now the widow Thornwell struggled against poverty, a battle that forced James to grow up too quickly. "We look for his boyhood," remarked a close friend, "and there is none." James was unusually emotional and never far from tears. Small and sickly, he made his health worse by smoking and chewing tobacco. To avoid punishment for misbehavior he often ran to the woods to hide, tiptoeing home only after dark. But punishment was postponed, not avoided. In the morning he invariably found his mother waiting for him with a switch. Family and friends were amazed at his love of school and addiction to reading. One night an accidental fire destroyed the neighborhood schoolhouse, including his little collection of books, and for weeks tears came to James' eyes whenever the loss was but mentioned.[4]

Once Dr. Graves, respected local physician, made a house call and noticed James with his head buried in a book as the other children played. Seeing that it was a volume of David Hume's *History of Great Britain*, Graves teased the boy, suggesting that he read something he could understand. James immediately thrust the book into the doctor's hands with a challenge to ask any question from it he wished. He did so and was astonished at the young scholar's mastery of what he had read. As they continued to talk, moving to other topics, the doctor's amazement grew. Graves would repeat the story as he traveled around the countryside until a planter named James Gillespie heard of young Thornwell. Gillespie and friend William Robbins, a lawyer from Cheraw, observed him for themselves and decided to share the expense of educating this most promising young man.[5]

Grateful for their benevolence and determined to make good, after attending local academies James chose to study at Thomas Cooper's South Carolina College. Examinations for admission were scheduled for early December 1829 and the seventeen year old fully expected to earn immediate placement in the junior class. "I was panic-struck as soon as I entered the library-room," confessed James in a letter to Mr. Robbins. He did well enough in most of the testing but was unprepared in mathematics and geometry and failed the exam. Crestfallen, he felt that he had let down his family and friends. "I am overwhelmed with confusion and ashamed to show my face." Though he could have begun as a sophomore, certainly no disgrace, he decided instead to make one more attempt. "I shall keep myself as much secluded as possible," he resolved, "until I redeem my reputation." After three weeks of intensive study he passed, entering the college as a junior in January 1830.

Thornwell described himself at this time as "hopelessly lean." One classmate remembered how a long coat nearly swallowed up the diminutive scholar. Another pictured Thornwell with "hands and face as thickly studded with black freckles as the Milky Way with stars." James had little time for the pranks and mischief of fellow students, though he did attend at least one drinking party. Out of a student body of one hundred and twenty he counted but seven "with whom I sometimes associate." So tightfisted was he with the money sent by lawyer Robbins that his benefactor once urged him to be more free spending! Young Thornwell developed a reputation as serious scholar, pushing himself to fourteen hours a day of what he termed "severe study." To polish English skills he memorized passages from Shakespeare, Milton, Edmund Burke and the King James Bible. On Saturdays he read history as recreation. It was the kind of regimen certain to impress his teachers. Dr. Cooper himself professed to see greatness in Thornwell's future, despite the young man's stubborn unionism and opposition to nullification. Thornwell wrote letters to the local newspaper and even authored a thirty-page pamphlet he felt contained "some strong arguments against Nullification."[6]

Thornwell most impressed his peers with an eloquence and combativeness in debate. "He could detect and expose a fallacy," remembered a classmate, "with more dispatch and completeness than I ever witnessed in any man." Thornwell was a member of the college's Euphradian Society, a literary and debating club, where oratory among student members reached new heights. Yet some of those he bested in debate may have thought he tried too hard. "His words burned like fire; his sarcasm was absolutely withering," said one. "He was admired for his tremendous abilities," according to a fellow student, "but not loved."[7]

Nineteen-year-old Thornwell graduated in December 1831, failed to secure the job he wanted as college librarian, accepting employment in Columbia as a tutor. He had raced through college, excelling in his studies, only to find himself underemployed and unsure of what to do with his life. In his depression he struggled with God. His mother's faith provided no answers to his nagging questions. "I can take you to the very spot," he said later, "where I stood and gnashed my teeth, and raised my hand, and said 'Well, I shall be damned, but...I am not to blame. God made me as I am, and I can't help my wickedness.'"

But God, it seemed, would not leave him alone. One spring day as he browsed through a bookstore he picked up a copy of the Puritan Reformers' *Westminster Confession of Faith*. Curious, he bought it, took it home and began reading. Overwhelmed by its logic, he read all through the night. Never, he felt, had he encountered a clearer distillation of scriptural doctrines. His mind continued to dwell on the claims of the gospel as he accepted a teaching position in Sumterville, South Carolina and there began attending nearby Concord Presbyterian Church. Before long he was ready to make a profession of faith and join the congregation. "I feel myself a weak, fallen, depraved and hopeless creature," he confessed to his Maker, "and utterly unable to do one righteous deed without Thy gracious assistance."[8]

Within a few months Thornwell had moved some fifty miles to become principal and teacher at Cheraw Academy. There he began to feel a call to the ministry and in November 1833 applied to Harmony Presbytery as a candidate. His preaching career almost ended before it began. The young man made such a poor impression that he was about to be rejected when one elder, perceiving a spark of promise, spoke up for him. The logical next step seemed to be a course of study at Columbia Theological Seminary in South Carolina's capital city. But in the spring of 1834 Dr. Ebenezer Porter, professor at renowned Andover Seminary, stopped in Cheraw after a visit to Columbia. Porter met Thornwell, sold him on the Congregationalist school and promised a scholarship.

That summer Thornwell began his studies in Massachusetts only to become quickly disillusioned. The foreign languages he hoped to learn were not being offered. And although Andover had a reputation for orthodoxy, Thornwell was convinced that they strayed from true Calvinism. Discovering that nearby Harvard Divinity School taught the courses he wanted in Hebrew and German, he transferred to Cambridge in the fall of 1834. He was appalled by the ubiquitous Unitarianism he found there. Robbins assured young Thornwell that his orthodox principles "withstood the insidious approaches of Dr. Cooper, and they cannot now give way to error, in a less dangerous form." The well-meaning liberals Thornwell met in Cambridge thought of themselves as "disciples of Jesus," but when questioned "they begin to recount certain doctrines of the Orthodox, and tell you very politely that they do *not* believe these." They seemed to reject the very foundations of the Christian faith, "and I do not know that the Bible holds out a solitary promise to a man for *not believing*."[9]

The would-be preacher had hoped to complete his language studies, then return home for further work at Columbia Theological Seminary. It was not to be. In precarious health, one doctor frankly warned Thornwell that the rigors of the approaching New England winter might kill him. Heeding the advice, in October he withdrew from Harvard and boarded a ship for South Carolina.

These few months had been instructive, despite the disappointments. A smile came to his face as he recalled the time he and a friend went to hear Edward Everett eulogize Lafayette. A vast multitude thronged Boston Common and filled Faneuil Hall. Pretending to be visiting dignitaries, the boys were directed to seats of honor next to John Quincy Adams and Daniel Webster. "A little impudence," Thornwell concluded, "is a great help in this world."[10]

Back in South Carolina Thornwell appeared again before Harmony Presbytery and this time, without reservation, was licensed to the ministry. He quickly took the pulpit of a new church with eighteen members in Lancasterville, South Carolina. Thornwell's little congregation was the first to experience what would later be described as "logic on fire," preaching that "wove garlands of beauty around discussions the most thorny and abstruse." One Sunday the young pastor preached for one and one-half hours, stopped, took out his watch and apologized for having lost track of the time. From around the sanctuary men spoke out, "Go on! Go on!," permitting him to preach an additional hour. Some years afterwards, preaching in Charleston on the Last Judgement, one hearer recounted how "the whole congregation appeared terror-stricken and unconsciously seized the back of the pews." One confessed to being "never so frightened." Over the years Webster, Calhoun, George Bancroft and Henry Ward Beecher would all come to praise his eloquence.[11]

Friend and fellow Presbyterian pastor Benjamin M. Palmer described Thornwell as having "one of those unfortunate faces that cannot be daguerreotyped." Every attempt "produced only a queer & grotesque caricature." Decades spent battling tuberculosis would leave their mark, yet not dampen an irrepressible sense of humor. Slim, of medium height, Thornwell had black hair and dark eyes that Palmer thought "capable of the utmost intensity of expression." Asked why he slept so late he would jokingly reply that man was meant to work at night and rest during the day. All through life Thornwell displayed a humility and geniality that drew people to him. "He is fond of a joke," said one associate, "tells a good one himself, and laughs heartily." Palmer once offered Thornwell a cigar. Taking a few critical puffs, he tossed it through an open window with the remark that "any man who will smoke such cigars will steal!" Palmer remembered that, "He was an inveterate tease, but only of those he loved."[12]

Thornwell started preaching in Lancasterville about the same time friend J. Marion Sims began his medical practice nearby. Sims yearned to marry a local girl named Theresa Jones but her mother opposed the match. Thornwell spoke to Mrs. Jones, a member of his church, and talked her into giving her consent. In the meantime Thornwell met Theresa's cousin, Nancy White Witherspoon, and fell in love with the young woman. Four years his senior, she was described as tall, of "large frame," yet "kind and loving" with "wonderful energy and vitality." Colonel Witherspoon at first demurred. No daughter of his, he grumbled, could survive on a preacher's salary. Yet he admired Thornwell and compared the young pastor intellectually to Calhoun and McDuffie. Reluctantly he gave his blessing and Nancy and James were married in December 1835.[13]

Thornwell would briefly pastor the little Presbyterian Church in Waxhaw, South Carolina, a few miles north of Lancasterville. Waxhaw was the village where a young Andrew Jackson had grown up. In 1837 Thornwell returned to Columbia, accepting a position at South Carolina College teaching courses in belles lettres, logic and metaphysics. It was rewarding work, but he soon missed his preaching ministry. After three semesters at the college he resigned to become pastor of the Presbyterian Church in South Carolina's capital.

In the pulpit Thornwell never preached from notes, but "wove his arguments in fire," a style one said combined "rigorous logic with strong emotion." After but one year as pastor church membership had doubled. But by 1840 he felt that God was leading him back to his alma mater. He submitted his resignation to the church and took up the duties of college chaplain as well as professor of sacred literature and the evidences of

Christianity. He was happy to be "entrusted with the care of souls" and looked forward to a fruitful ministry among the college boys.[14]

Thornwell was in charge of daily chapel services at South Carolina College and he also found time to lead a Bible study, hold prayer meetings and preach on Sundays. As a professor he was never too busy or aloof to answer students' questions, though he demanded much. "Dr. Thornwell is the only teacher," one student complained, "for whose recitation I can never say I am fully prepared." Thornwell believed in hard work and required it from others, emphasizing the need "to preserve our virtues from the rust of idleness." After all, he would add, "Few men can be unoccupied and innocent at the same time." Methodical self-discipline governed his life and he encouraged it in his students. "Habit," he was wont to tell them, "is the effect of a succession of the same acts."[15]

Not long after his return to the campus Thornwell's tuberculosis worsened and a sea voyage was prescribed. In May of 1841 he set sail for Europe, leaving Nancy and two young children at home. The salt air seemed to help and he spent the next several weeks traveling through England and Scotland, awed by magnificent cathedrals and surrounded by history. His spirits soared in this environment but he began to miss home. Writing to Nancy from London he could only conclude "that in all that makes life precious, and exalts, refines, and elevates the mass of the people, America is immeasurably superior to England." By the time he reached Paris in July his patriotism was irrepressible. "I candidly believe that America is the first nation on the globe," he wrote, "and all through the continent of Europe the American flag is honored and respected...I am proud of my nation and prouder still after having seen others."

Soon, his health and outlook improved, he was sailing home. Leaving Charlotte, North Carolina on the last stage of his journey he tried to make himself comfortable as the horse-drawn coach rumbled down the highway. Crossing finally into South Carolina Thornwell's emotions overcame him. He leaped from the carriage, knelt there on the ground and kissed the soil of the Palmetto State.[16]

II.

Southerners had long accepted slavery as a natural component of American republicanism, just as slavery had been the cornerstone of the historical republics of Greece, Carthage and Rome. Moreover, slavery was argued to be ultimately conducive to liberty in that it controlled potentially disruptive individuals, defused conflict between capital and labor and promoted equality within the ruling class. John Locke, English champion of natural rights, made provision for slavery in his political theories. When Southerners studied history they encountered slavery in every ancient civilization, defended by sages and philosophers from Aristotle to Augustine.

When they opened their Bibles they learned of slavery among the Hebrew people, sanctioned and regulated by the law God gave to Moses. Slaves in New Testament times were admonished by Paul to obey their masters even as the Apostle sent one runaway back to his owner. The founders of American liberty, giants such as Washington, Jefferson and Madison—all were slave owners. Southerners born into this way of life, heirs to a tradition as old as the human race, not surprisingly looked with suspicion on those bent on bringing down the institution. When the most moderate of Northern reformers conceded that slavery might be a national problem the entire country ought to bear the expense of ending, many Southerners bristled at even this suggestion of interference.[17] To the strident demands and bloodthirsty rhetoric of the more militant abolitionists, Southerners reacted with fury and disgust.

"The tories here have a prodigious prejudice against us, and abolitionism is, if possible, more fanatical here than in America," wrote Thornwell during his stay in London.[18] What especially disturbed him was that spirit of antislavery extremism that excused any crime or excess that might be committed in the name of freedom. This new abolitionist movement was like a venomous serpent, growing stronger and more dangerous every year, until now even the church seemed threatened.

Though any sort of antislavery sentiment seldom found favor among Deep South churchmen, in the Upper South emancipation had long had many thoughtful advocates. As far back as 1818 the Lexington, Virginia Presbytery urged Christians to terminate the institution through "their honest, earnest, and unwearied endeavors." Two decades later Presbyterian emancipationists in the Old Dominion were criticizing both slavery and that violent new creed called abolitionism. By the time Thornwell entered the ministry zealots within his denomination had begun demanding the passage of antislavery resolutions. Conservatives responded by denying the church's authority to legislate on the subject. When the Presbyterian General Assembly of 1836 chose to postpone rather than declare an end to antislavery agitation many predicted outright schism. The *Southern Religious Telegraph* of Richmond feared that continued warfare over slavery within the Presbyterian Church would drive Southerners out. "Let no one construe these remarks into a defense of slavery," cautioned the editor. "Christians, and our citizens generally, view it as a great evil. But the remedy for it prescribed by abolitionists is worse, incomparably worse, than the disease."[19]

For his part, Thornwell had little patience with those calling themselves "Christian abolitionists." Such people, he said, having determined that slavery must be sinful, run to the Bible searching for support. They quote some "maxim of universal benevolence," ignoring the rest of Scripture, then point their finger at slavery and pronounce it in violation. If the Golden Rule made slave ownership a sin, Thornwell asked, could not identical logic be used to condemn private property or even marriage? "The same line of argument, carried out precisely in the same way, would make havoc with all the institutions of civilized society."

For Thornwell the Bible was the only rule of faith and sole standard of morality. And he found nothing there to condemn slavery. If slavery be sin, "it is truly amazing that the Bible, which professes to be a lamp to our feet and a light to our path, to make the man of God perfect, thoroughly furnished unto every good work, nowhere gives the slightest caution against this tremendous evil." The Word of God regulates slavery, as it does other human relationships, without condemning it. "We find masters exhorted in the same connection with husbands, parents, magistrates; slaves exhorted in the same connection with children and subjects." One early New Testament church, Thornwell pointed out, was organized in the home of the slaveholder Philemon, a man Paul addresses as "our dearly beloved, and fellow labourer" and commends for his Christian virtues. "Admit the principle," Thornwell argued, "that slavery, essentially considered, is not a sin, and the injunctions of Scripture are plain, consistent, intelligible; deny the principle, and the Bible seems to be made up of riddles."[20]

Abolitionists who call themselves Christians, in their zeal to attack slavery, "are striking at the foundation of our common faith" when they misquote the Bible or reject its authority. "If men," warned Thornwell, "are free from their own heads to frame systems of morality, which render null and void the commandments of God, we see not why they are not equally at liberty to frame systems of doctrines, which render vain the covenant of grace." Slavery, he concluded, "may be opposed upon considerations of policy and prudence." Emancipation is a "political question" over which "communities and States may honestly differ." But as long as the Bible is the supreme arbiter of right and wrong, slavery may not be branded as sinful. What, asked the preacher, is the meaning of "freedom" to an unsaved person who is himself a slave to sin? Thornwell preached a spiritual emancipation that went beyond the circumstances of earthly existence, "a freedom enjoyed by the martyr at the stake, the slave in his chains, the prisoner in his dungeon, as well as the king upon his throne."[21]

He argued that slavery was an institution "implicated in every fibre of Southern Society," and that continued agitation on the question would not only divide the church but eventually bring down the country. Northern Christians must understand what was at stake. "We do not ask them to patronize Slavery; we do not wish them to change their own institutions; we only ask them to treat us as the Apostles treated the slaveholders of their day, and leave us the liberty, which we accord to them, of conducting our affairs according to our own convictions of truth and duty."[22]

Northerners calling for an immediate end to Southern slavery seemed to forget the long history of bondage in their own states. For generations African slaves had toiled in each of the thirteen American colonies, purchased from other Africans and brought in chains to the New World in the holds of New England slave ships. Pennsylvania's experience was instructive. There, long before independence, the Quaker-dominated assembly recognized slavery and codified a rigorous system of race control. William Penn himself owned a dozen black slaves and is said to have preferred them to indentured whites because slave labor was permanent. In colonial days some Quakers expressed misgivings, but most readily accepted slavery.

Only gradually did antislavery sentiment grow until finally there arose a serious movement to end it. Benjamin Franklin eventually cast his lot with Pennsylvania's emancipationists, though he owned as many as five blacks at one time and never got around to freeing any. During the American Revolution many Pennsylvania slaves ran away, some joining the Tory cause, lured by promises of freedom should Britain win the war. In 1780 the Pennsylvania legislature passed the Gradual Abolition Act, the first such statute in America. By its provisions all slaves born before March first of that year remained slaves for life, while children born to slaves after that date would be set free after twenty-eight years of servitude. This meant that there would be slaves in the Keystone State until 1847.[23] But emancipation had been officially legislated with little social disturbance or economic cost.

Alexis de Tocqueville observed that when Northern masters were faced with the imminent prospect of having to let go of their slaves they often sold them to new owners in states where slavery still existed. "Consequently," observed the Frenchman, "the abolition of slavery does not make the slave free but just changes his master to a southerner instead of a northerner." Southerners inclined to consider emancipation had fewer practical choices, in de Tocqueville's view. "The North rids itself of slavery and of the slaves in one move. In the South there is no hope of attaining this double result at the same time."[24]

Slavery seemed uniquely suited to Southern agriculture. Worldwide demand made cotton America's number one export, production growing from a mere three thousand bales in 1790 to four million by 1860. As cotton acreage spread, so did slavery. Farmers in the North might require extra help to sow and harvest, but their wheat, corn and other grains demanded few hands at other times. The Southern staples of cotton and tobacco needed almost continual care by many workers through a long season. Yet there was inefficiency in tying up capital in a labor force that must be clothed and fed year-round. "While the farmers of Ohio and Illinois," observed one historian, "were obtaining white laborers on wages to be paid from current earnings and were investing their profits in land improvements, railroads and local factories, the planters of Alabama and Louisiana were applying their cash and straining their credit to buy slaves whose lifetime labor must be paid for in advance."[25]

Slavery had other costs more difficult to measure. According to de Tocqueville, writing in the aftermath of Nat Turner's abortive 1831 slave insurrection, the specter of revolt haunted the Southern mind. Northerners, secure from danger themselves, freely discussed the prospect of a race war drowning the South in blood. Below the Mason and Dixon Line the nightmare was not dealt with so openly. "In the southern states there is silence," said de Tocqueville, "one does not speak of the future before strangers; one avoids discussing it with one's friends; each man, so to say, hides it from himself. There is something more frightening about the silence of the South than about the North's noisy fears." Three-fourths of Southern whites had no proprietary stake in slavery, in that neither they nor their immediate family owned slaves. Still, the entire South was tied to the institution that many were coming to view as a bulwark of civilization itself.[26]

With abolitionists calling for slavery's violent overthrow, Southern reaction to threatened terrorism was predictable. "The abolitionist is as free to hold his opinions as I am to hold mine," said Randolph of Roanoke. "But I will never suffer him to put a torch to my property, that he may slake it in the blood of all that are dear to me." Randolph labeled slavery a "cancer," but one that "must not be tampered with by quacks, who never saw the disease or the patient."

When Randolph died his slaves were freed, sent to farms purchased for them in the free state of Ohio under the terms of his will. There they were met by mob violence and forced to flee. Yet it was incessant abolitionist propaganda that demonized Southerners and pictured their country as fit only for destruction. "If Northern abolition action has goaded and driven us to be *also* fanatical," claimed Virginia's Edmund Ruffin, "our fanaticism has been, and is altogether defensive." Thornwell categorized abolitionism as but one of many modern "isms," a manifestation of "a general spirit of madness" growing in nineteenth-century America. "It is a hot, boiling, furious fanaticism, destroying all energy of mind and symmetry of character and leaving its unfortunate victim...a spectacle of pity and of dread."[27]

Not that Thornwell was blind to the evils of slavery. Though he tried to be an ideal master himself he never idealized the institution. "Slavery," said the preacher, "is a part of the curse which sin has introduced into the world, and stands in the same general relations to Christianity as poverty, sickness, disease or death." In Heaven the picture of the slave would be as impossible as that of one crippled or blind. "That there are abuses connected with the institution may be freely and honestly conceded," he went on, "but let it be remembered that in this fallen world...the nearest, tenderest, holiest relations of life are liable to enormous perversions..." In Thornwell's understanding of Providence there could be no utopian solution, no lifting of the curse of sin by human efforts. Man's only hope was the gospel. He

felt a deep responsibility for evangelizing the slaves and saw great oppor-
tunities to make converts among them. That bondmen might learn to read
the Bible, Thornwell advocated repeal of South Carolina's seldom-enforced
law against teaching slaves to read. "Our design in giving them the Gospel,"
said Thornwell, "is not to civilize them, not to change their social condition; not to exalt them into citizens or freemen; it is to save them."[28]

There were those who wondered if Thornwell's intellect and communication skills might have been better used in the political arena, arguing
the South's case before the rest of the country. John C. Calhoun met
Thornwell on at least two occasions and went away comparing him to his
old teacher, the revered Timothy Dwight of Yale. "I was not prepared," the
senator went on to say, "for the thorough acquaintance he exhibited with
all the topics that are generally familiar only to statesmen." As the church,
in Thornwell's view, must avoid political entanglements so must the state
have no jurisdiction over matters of faith. "But the separation of Church
and State," Thornwell added, "is a very different thing from the separation
of religion and the State." Lawmakers and magistrates may properly conform legislation and governmental conduct to the teachings of the Bible
without violating in the least the Constitution's proscription of "an establishment of religion."[29] However it was not his political views but his insistence on the authority of Scripture in both theology and church polity that
earned Thornwell the sobriquet "the Calhoun of the Church."

A friend said of Thornwell that "he bowed with perfect docility before the dogmatic authority of the Scripture." Only the Bible, the revealed
and perfect Word of God, set forth eternal and unchangeable standards of
duty, morality and truth. The church, in Thornwell's words, "has a fixed
and unalterable Constitution; and that Constitution is the Word of God."
He was confident that Christians would always have a positive influence
on any society in which they lived. But the evils brought on by the fall of
man were beyond the power or duty of the church to set right. "The Bible,
and the Bible alone, is her rule of faith and practice. She can announce
what it teaches, enjoin what it commands, prohibit what it condemns, and
enforce her testimonies by spiritual sanctions. Beyond the Bible she can
never go, and apart from the Bible she can never speak." The church exer-
cises only spiritual authority and must never involve itself with any political party or cause, however worthy it may seem. The church, said Thornwell,
"has a *creed*, but no *opinions*."[30]

Presbyterians were about to tackle that very issue. As a young pastor
Thornwell had attended his first General Assembly in 1837. That year the
Presbyterian Church was divided between adherents of a moderate Calvinism referred to as "New School" and the more traditional orthodoxy of
the "Old School." There were other issues involved, and slavery played a
peripheral role, but the Old School victory in that assembly could be cred-
ited to the determination of delegates to hold true to their church's distinctive

doctrines. Young Thornwell voted with the majority though he took no active part. In succeeding years his stature and reputation grew, as did the respect of even his adversaries. "Whenever he was present in the Assembly," remembered fellow pastor and outspoken abolitionist Henry Ward Beecher, "he was always the first person pointed out to a stranger."[31]

In May of 1845 the annual meeting was held in Cincinnati, a city on the border between slave and non-slaveholding states. Presbyterian abolitionists continued to insist that slave ownership ought to constitute a ban to communion. A committee of seven was chosen to study the subject and bring a report before the entire assembly. Thornwell's verbal opinion was solicited and he also wrote a paper for the committee explaining his views and their basis in Scripture. Writing to his wife, Thornwell characterized the assembly as one of "harmony, courtesy, and Christian feeling." He hoped that the committee, and in turn the assembly, would hold slavery "not to be sinful, will assert that it is sanctified by the word of God, that it is purely a civil relation, with which the Church, as such, has no right to interfere, and that abolitionism is essentially wicked, disorganizing, and ruinous."

He was not to be disappointed. The final resolution that passed, by a better than twelve-to-one margin, declared that the church "cannot legislate where Christ has not legislated, nor make terms of membership which he has not made." The very language echoed Thornwell's. "[S]ince Christ and his inspired Apostles did not make the holding of slaves a ban to communion, we, as a court of Christ, have no authority to do so; since they did not attempt to remove it from the church by legislation, we have no authority on the subject."[32] Through the stormy years ahead the Presbyterian Church could now stand above the national debate over slavery. Even as Methodists and Baptists split in the face of antislavery agitation, Presbyterians held together for the next sixteen years in peace and a surprising unity.

He never made much of the victory, nor did he boast of his part in the outcome, but the triumph was Thornwell's. Leaving Cincinnati, he traveled by stagecoach and railroad to Baltimore, all along the way marveling at the beauty of the country. "The more I reflect on the subject," he wrote to his wife from Wheeling, Virginia, "the more I am satisfied that the mission of our Republic will not be accomplished, until we embrace in our Union the whole of this North American continent." His dream, he confessed to Nancy, was nothing less than "a grand imperial Republic" that God might use to "accomplish great purposes." Oregon must be held; California, Texas and perhaps even Mexico added to the Union. And what if New England should "kick up a dust" over acquisition of the slaveholding Republic of Texas? "If the Yankees feel disposed to leave us," he wrote, "let them go; but the West and the South can never be separated." In his view it was, after all, parochial New England that perennially stood in the way of national unity and greatness. "There is," he concluded, "at work in this land, a Yankee spirit, and an American spirit; and the latter must triumph."[33]

III.

"All passions fatal to a republic," de Tocqueville had written, "grow with the increase of its territory..." Any such concern was far from the mind of President Jefferson when he seized the opportunity to purchase the vast Louisiana Territory from Napoleon Bonaparte in 1803. Objections raised about the legality of the acquisition Republicans had little trouble answering.[34] But over the years other disputes had arisen involving the new land, issues of slavery, constitutional interpretation and sectionalism that defied settlement.

Louisiana, formerly the Territory of Orleans, became in 1812 the eighteenth star in America's flag, the first state to be formed out of those lands purchased from France. Six years later the territorial legislature of Missouri asked for admission. The House of Representatives in Washington approved, but attached an amendment requiring that Missouri phase out slavery after statehood. The Senate balked at such a stipulation. The Constitution, insisted John Taylor, allowed Congress to *admit* new states, not *make* states. Jefferson saw Northern sectionalism conspiring to keep additional Southern states out of the Union. The question of slavery carried with it, according to the former president, "just enough semblance of morality to throw dust into the eyes of the people, & to fanaticize them; while with the knowing ones it is simply a question of power." When Maine applied for statehood in December 1819 a Senate-House conference committee proposed a bargain. Both states would be admitted, Missouri retaining the right of property in slaves. But slavery would be banned from all remaining territory of the Louisiana Purchase above the latitude 36°30' north, Missouri's southern border.[35]

Southern opinion was divided on the proposed compromise. Most agreed that while Congress might accept or reject applications for statehood, no conditions for entry had existed for the original states and none could properly be imposed now. "Missouri has no right to compel Maine to admit of slavery," said Taylor, "nor Maine any right to compel Missouri to prohibit it, because each state has a right to think for itself." Madison argued that slaveowners had the right to travel throughout the Union with their slaves, and that Congress possessed no authority to keep slavery out of territory belonging to the United States. Most Southerners, however, acquiesced in the assumption that Congress might prohibit slavery in the territories, a concession they would later regret. Charles Pinckney of South Carolina had been a member of the Constitutional Convention and he reminded the House of Representatives that the framers never intended that Congress involve itself in slavery. He feared setting a precedent now. Warnings were not heeded as the House, by a narrow margin, passed Speaker Henry Clay's compromise. "But this is a reprieve only, not a final solution," predicted Jefferson. "A geographical line coinciding with a marked principle—moral and political—once conceived and held up to the angry passions of man, will not be obliterated; and every new irritation will make it deeper and deeper."[36]

As antislavery agitation divided the country, Jefferson could only characterize the institution itself as a curse on both master and bondman. Many others of the revolutionary generation had difficulty reconciling the Declaration's "self-evident truths" with the reality of slavery. Men like prominent Connecticut lawyer Theodore Dwight, even in the first years of the Republic, were deeply offended by the existence of slavery in America. "And since the mighty, and majestic course of Freedom has begun," concluded Dwight, "nothing but the arm of Omnipotence can prevent it from reaching to the miserable Africans." Jefferson's mind kept returning to the myriad problems—economic, social and political—that freedom must bring. "Nothing is more certainly written in the book of fate than that these people are to be free," prophesied the sage of Monticello, "nor is it less certain that the two races, equally free, cannot live in the same government."[37]

As America entered the nineteenth century religion increasingly came to define the antislavery cause, one result of that outburst of revivalism called the Second Great Awakening. Characterized by sometimes extreme emotionalism and an emphasis on "good works," orthodox Calvinists decried the shift in theology towards Arminianism. Many evangelicals, such as famed revivalist Charles G. Finney, felt slavery violated Christian principles found in the spirit if not the letter of Scripture. Unitarian minister Theodore Parker took much the same stand based on the dictates of conscience, his admitted "last standard of appeal."[38] In any case, to confess that slavery was immoral left little room for compromise or concession.

Yet even among those marching in the ranks of the antislavery crusade, few believed in racial equality, despite accusations thrown at them by their enemies. The Declaration of Independence's oft-quoted axiom "that all men are created equal" was not meant by its author and signers to apply to African bondmen. Even as black racial inferiority was an underlying assumption that bolstered slavery, many Northerners came to oppose the institution, and its spread westward, on the same grounds. Would the "unexplored and almost interminable regions beyond the Mississippi," asked Rhode Island Senator James Burrill, be settled by "free white men" or "by slaves, and blackened with their continually increasing progeny?" The junior senator from Providence left no doubt as to where he stood. "I am not only adverse to a slave population, but also to any population composed of blacks, and of the infinite and motley confusion of colors between the black and the white."[39]

For all parties the annexation of Texas had been bound up inextricably with the issue of slavery's expansion. To Southerners, outvoted in the House of Representatives and barely hanging on to equality in the Senate, the admission of the Republic of Texas seemed their last, best hope. Most Texans wanted to join the American Union. Abolitionists were, of course, bitterly opposed. Southern success would eventually come in the aftermath of a bizarre tragedy.

On a February afternoon in 1844 President John Tyler, cabinet ministers, legislators and a large party of guests were enjoying a cruise on the Potomac River aboard the new steam-powered warship *Princeton*. The president was below, happily conversing with a group of ladies. As the vessel passed Mount Vernon the proud captain ordered a salute in honor of George Washington. The gun to be fired was nicknamed the "Peacemaker," largest weapon in the fleet. No problems had appeared during tests. But this time the great gun exploded, throwing deadly shrapnel into the crowd of seamen and civilians on deck. Killed instantly was Secretary of State Abel P. Upshur, Navy Secretary Thomas W. Gilmer, Senator David Gardiner and five others. Eleven more were injured.

Even as the bodies of the victims lay in state in the East Room, former Congressman Henry Wise of Virginia arrived breathless at the White House. Secretary Upshur had labored for Texas' annexation and seemed to have the votes needed in the Senate, though details remained to be worked out with President Sam Houston. Now, pleaded Wise, the vacancy in the State Department must be filled by John C. Calhoun. Thinking Calhoun's name might unnecessarily link Texas annexation with slavery's expansion, Tyler was reluctant. Wise then blurted out that he had made it clear to Calhoun that Tyler wanted him for the position. Frustrated and angry at his friend's presumptuousness, the president went ahead and sent the nomination to the Senate. Within hours, without referring the nomination to committee, unanimous consent was given.[40]

Calhoun felt that Texas could well be the last slave state admitted. The security of the South would be bolstered, however, by the understanding that Texas might in the future be divided into as many as six states. From mass meetings across the South in the spring of 1844 came cries for annexation. "We hold it to be better out of the Union with Texas," proclaimed one resolution from Williamsburg District, South Carolina, "than in it without her."[41] Despite Northern fears stirred by Secretary of State Calhoun's openly avowed intentions, few could resist the appeal of American expansion. Texas was a jewel that must be possessed. A joint resolution was finally passed by both houses of Congress and signed by the president, providing for statehood. The incoming Polk administration would finalize the deal, but Calhoun and Tyler could take a measure of credit for adding Texas's star to the flag.

In the spring of 1846 there arose from every corner of the land a cry for war. Mexican troops had crossed the Rio Grande and were advancing onto American soil!

Just months before there were hopes of peacefully resolving differences between the two countries. President James K. Polk dispatched John Slidell to the Mexican capital to negotiate a long-standing border dispute and even make an offer to purchase California and that vast expanse of western land known simply as New Mexico. But soon after Slidell's arrival in Mexico City the government was overthrown and the new army-backed dictatorship ordered him out of the country. Polk quickly sent troops to the Rio Grande border. Mexican authorities, claiming land hundreds of miles to the east, responded by declaring war on April 23 and marching their soldiers into the disputed territory. Skirmishes followed and American blood was shed.

Young volunteers rallied to the Stars and Stripes as patriotic fervor swept the country North and South. Mexico must be punished and made to release her hold on the western lands! Few doubted America's divine mandate to build "an empire for liberty," and a rapid succession of battlefield victories made conquest of Mexico a certainty. John L. O'Sullivan seemed to capture the idea when he coined the phrase "manifest destiny" to describe what he saw as a plan ordained by God for expansion across the continent. Only a handful bothered to dissent, mostly abolitionists fearful that territory gained from Mexico would be opened to slavery.

Almost alone among Southern leaders, South Carolina Senator John C. Calhoun opposed the war. As secretary of state he had been instrumental in securing, just months before, the admission of Texas as America's twenty-eighth state. The acquisition had been made despite vociferous complaints from abolitionists and Calhoun realized that the North would never allow slavery's expansion into land that might be won from Mexico. The conquest of new western territories could only deepen sectional divisions. Calhoun also questioned Polk's diplomatic and military maneuvering. The president, Calhoun charged, had in effect usurped Congress's war-making authority by actions that deliberately brought on a fight. Such a constitutional violation was "monstrous." Still, when the House passed the declaration of war, the Senate went along despite his pleading.[42]

Once committed to combat, Calhoun supported American forces and hoped for a quick victory. When the invaders were repelled and the Rio Grande secured he insisted that a continuation of the bloodletting was inexcusable. War for the purpose of expansion was not what the Founding Fathers intended for America. Only as peacemaker could the United States promote liberty and hold her head high as an example around the world.[43]

That summer there came an event that shocked Southerners out of their complacency even as it confirmed Calhoun's fears. Young David Wilmot, Democrat from Towanda, Pennsylvania, rose from his desk to offer a simple amendment to a House appropriations bill. The congressman and his supporters were fed up with what they saw as Southern domination of the party and of national affairs. He proposed that slavery be banned from any territory conquered from Mexico. "The negro race," he said, "already occupy enough of this fair continent..."[44]

Southerners were stunned. What right, they asked, did the federal government have to take sides on the slavery issue? Was not the government the agent of the Southern as well as the Northern states? Were not the territories the common property of both? Had not Southern blood been shed in the war with Mexico? Wilmot's proviso passed the House of Representatives but ran into sufficient opposition to fail in the Senate. The damage had been done, although Northerners could not understand the South's reaction. Restricting slavery seemed a reasonable and worthy goal. Southerners saw it as a "slap in the face," a virtual declaration of war by a people supposed to be fellow countrymen.

Calhoun believed that sectional conflict over slavery in the territories would bring the Union crashing down. "I desire above all things to save the whole," he wrote privately, "but if that cannot be, to save the portion where Providence has cast my lot." As a reaffirmation of Southern determination Calhoun introduced resolutions in the Senate proclaiming the territories to be the joint property of the states, denying Congress's power to deprive the states of their rights in these common lands. Principle was at stake. A year later Calhoun refused to support a resolution introduced by Henry Clay explicitly permitting slavery in the territories. Congress, insisted Calhoun, had no more right to permit slavery than it did to prohibit it.[45]

Florida had been admitted in March 1845, the final Southern state to enter the Union. The following year Iowa and Wisconsin came in. North and South each had fifteen states. To end the strife over which section would prevail in the territories, Senator Henry Clay backed a plan he hoped might go even further, settling forever the slavery issue and its threat to the Union. Under his proposal the buying and selling of slaves in the District of Columbia would end and California would be admitted as a non-slaveholding state, tipping the sectional balance finally against the South. In return for these concessions the territories of New Mexico and Utah would be opened to settlers with or without slaves. Most importantly, the South was assured that the Constitution's provision for returning runaways would at last be effectively enforced. After furious debate the entire package, called the Compromise Measures of 1850, was passed by Congress and signed into law. Southern secessionists warned that compromise only postponed the inevitable separation. Abolitionists continued to denounce any accommodation with slavery and excoriated those who voted for peace.

One of James Madison's arguments for ratification of the Constitution had been that a stronger Union would improve security for slavery. The new Constitution required that states return fugitive slaves to their owners, something neglected in the old Articles of Confederation. "This is better security than any that now exists," argued Madison. "No power," he went on to assure, "is given to the general government to interpose with respect to the property in slaves now held by the states." It was said that the Fugitive Slave Law would now finally put teeth in this constitutional promise. Senator Rhett was less hopeful. This "concession" by the North, to obey the Constitution, would still be almost unenforceable in that section.[46]

Just as he feared, abolitionists inflamed mobs to take the law into their own hands, often overpowering law officers and freeing apprehended runaways. State after state in the North passed "personal liberty laws" designed to circumvent (if not explicitly nullify) the federal legislation. Northern governors routinely refused extradition requests. The compromise, designed to end sectional squabbling over slavery, was proving to be a bitter disappointment.

Daniel Webster had suffered shrill criticism from abolitionists for his support of the compromise. No friend of slavery, he opposed the annexation of Texas and war with Mexico. But, like Calhoun, he loved the Union. Speaking on Independence Day 1851 the Massachusetts senator issued a solemn warning to slavery's fanatical foes. Should the Northern states continue "willfully and deliberately" to circumvent federal law, "the South would no longer be bound to observe the [constitutional] compact." His very use of the word "compact" to describe the Constitution was enough to startle friend and foe. "A bargain cannot be broken on one side," said the old Federalist, "and still bind the other side."[47]

———

In October of 1845, just months after his triumph at the Cincinnati General Assembly, Thornwell was called to the pastorate of Baltimore's Second Presbyterian Church. He accepted, resigned his professorship at South Carolina College and began to make arrangements for the move, even selling his furniture. Rather than lose him, college trustees invoked a seldom-used law requiring he give a twelve-month notice. Thornwell felt that obedience to the law, however inconvenient, was a moral obligation. He would remain for the time being at his Columbia teaching post, still taking an active part in denominational affairs. The 1847 General Assembly elected him its moderator, at age 34 the youngest in history, but he still dreamed of again pastoring a church. During a pleasant stay in Lancasterville in late summer 1850 Thornwell wrote of dreading the time "when we must go back to the walls of our prison. College is to me like a dungeon; and I go to its duties like a slave whipped to his burden."[48]

The following spring he received the call of another church and this time the trustees relented. The pulpit he would fill was that of Glebe Street Presbyterian Church in Charleston. "Pungent and searching evangelistic preaching is much needed in this city," Thornwell soon discovered. "Fine houses, splendid organs, fashionable congregations, — these seem to be the rage. It is not asked, *what* a man preaches; but *where* he preaches, and to *whom*." The new pastor rolled up his sleeves to do battle with worldliness and complacency. "This state of feeling I am anxious to see thoroughly undermined and broken up.[49]

Thornwell was not unacquainted with the great city. The previous year he had come to Charleston to deliver the dedicatory sermon at Zion Church in the Ansonborough District. Built by white Presbyterians and Episcopalians for the use of a black congregation, some Charlestonians had opposed its construction. A mob once threatened to destroy the half-completed structure. But on May 26, 1850 Thornwell preached to a white audience gathered to dedicate the building.

His text was verse one of the fourth chapter of Colossians: "Masters, give unto your servants that which is just and equal; knowing that ye also have a Master in heaven." The building of churches for blacks, said Thornwell, was the very best response Christian slaveholders could make to abolitionists. Zion Church stood as a testimony to his belief that "the Negro is of one blood with ourselves, that he has sinned as we have, and that he has an equal interest with us in the great redemption." Some had begun to quote science in support of racial theories that denied humanity to blacks. Others supposed a separate creation of the black race. Such speculation Thornwell rejected as contrary to Scripture and therefore heretical. There must be no departure from the Word of God. In the black Thornwell recognized one who "has within him a soul of priceless value," an individual created in the image of God. "We are not ashamed," he said, "to call him our *brother*."

Did slavery violate the rule of Jesus that his followers love others as they love themselves? If such were admitted, reasoned Thornwell, how would we apply the principle to other areas of life? To be utterly consistent "the judge would not condemn the criminal, nor the executioner behead him; the rich man could not claim his possessions nor the poor learn patience from their sufferings." Abolitionists claimed that no man had the right to own another, that such a system made the bondman a thing and not a person. Not so, answered Thornwell. "The right which the master has is a right, not to the man, but to his *labor*..." A Northern worker performs his job "in consequence of a contract" while slave labor "is rendered in consequence of a command." Only the principle is different. "The labourers in each case are equally moral, equally responsible, equally men." All of the Southern states have laws to protect slaves, he continued, safeguards admittedly less than perfect. But the institution cannot be condemned for its abuses. "When slavery is pronounced to be essentially sinful, the argument cannot turn upon incidental circumstances of the system, upon the defective arrangements of the details, the inadequate securities which the law awards...it must turn upon the nature of the relation itself..." The chastisement of a slave is not necessarily cruel. "All that is necessary...is that the punishment be *just*."[50]

Thornwell had been pastoring in the Port City but six months when word came that William Campbell Preston, president of South Carolina College, had resigned due to ill health. Almost immediately the trustees met and invited Thornwell to return to Columbia as the school's sixth president. It was a great honor, but he felt an obligation to the church he had only begun to serve. He would let his congregation make the decision, though "the people cannot speak upon the subject without bursting into tears." Reluctantly, they voted to let him go.[51]

Soon after President Thornwell settled into his new job, tragedy struck. Two-year-old Mary Elizabeth, his youngest daughter, suddenly took ill and died. He and Nancy buried her next to their baby girl who had died fourteen years before. The grieving Thornwell never questioned his God. "I feel that my child has blessed me in her death, though it was denied her to bless me by her life."[52]

Despite the family's bereavement, a trip had been planned to New England and Thornwell felt it was important he go. He would visit college campuses, learn what he could of their educational methods and perhaps promote goodwill. At Harvard University he attended commencement, was treated with deference and came away impressed with the venerable institution. A lack of orthodox faith still concerned him. "But it must be confessed that Boston is a great city," he wrote to his wife. "There are things about it that make you proud of it as an American city." At Yale University, the alma mater of John C. Calhoun, he sought to soothe sectional feeling with diplomatic words. "I was never more kindly treated than I have been here," he reported to Nancy from New Haven. "I rejoice that in letters, as in religion, there is neither North nor South, East nor West."[53]

———

Sectionalism remained very much alive in the never-ending struggle over the territories. In 1854 Illinois Democrat Stephen A. Douglas sponsored a bill to organize the region called Nebraska, that sprawling land remaining from the Louisiana Purchase. The senator expected that settlement of this area would bring the transcontinental railroad through the Midwest rather than the South. To gain Southern support for what became known as the Kansas-Nebraska Act, Douglas and his allies proposed to repeal the Missouri Compromise's geographic restriction on slavery. There would be a new principle. Northern Democrats were delighted to embrace what they called "popular sovereignty" — the right of a territory's settlers to accept or reject slavery for themselves. Abolitionists were outraged that this "squatter sovereignty" might open new land to slavery. Southerners agreed that the people of a territory should be the ones to decide, but only when they were admitted to the Union. Until then a territory was the common property of the states and the federal government, as their agent, could not take sides by banning slavery. After all, the Fifth

Amendment guaranteed that "No person shall...be deprived of life, liberty, or property, without due process of law..." Since slave labor was a form of property, for the federal government to abolish slavery in a territory would be to destroy property without compensation, violating the due process clause. Territorial legislatures, created as they were by Congress, could exercise no power not possessed by their creator.[54]

Turmoil caused by the controversy drove a wedge more deeply between North and South and created disarray in the ranks of Whigs and Democrats. The new American Party seemed to some to offer hope of national unity. As much a secret society as it was political party, when asked about their activities members habitually answered "I know nothing." This "Know Nothing" Party opposed the flood of immigration, especially German and Irish Catholics, that was pouring into the big cities of the North. Foreign immigration was hardly a concern in the Deep South, but Thornwell thought he saw in the American Party "the only organization which, in my judgement, can save the country from impending ruin." He was not active and told but a few friends of his feeble partisan foray. "You know," he confided to a friend, "that I always was perverse in politics."[55]

College trustees must have shook their heads as Thornwell tendered his resignation as president at the end of November 1854. This time he had anticipated their opposition. In accordance with the law he would stay on for a full year; his new employer, Columbia Theological Seminary, prepared to wait for him. It would be a sacrifice in salary and prestige to become professor of didactic and polemic theology at the tiny seminary. But he felt he was wasting time and energy on the routine of college administration. Still, no one was ever more influential with the students.[56]

Thornwell's leadership was legendary. On one occasion two unprepared scholars were admitted to the college on condition they later retake the admission test. When they made a spectacular failure of the second exam the professor in charge became livid and demanded their suspension or expulsion. The angry pedagogue turned to President Thornwell for support, who until then had remained quietly in the background. "These young gentlemen were admitted on a certain condition," Thornwell replied, "this condition has not been fulfilled; consequently they are not members of the college. You cannot expel or suspend them without recognizing them as members." He would give them one more month to study and if they appeared again unprepared they would simply be denied admission.

A more serious episode occurred some months after he left the college. Thornwell was delivering a seminary lecture when the classroom door burst open. He must come quickly! Two hundred South Carolina College students, outraged over an alleged incident of police brutality, had armed themselves with muskets and were confronting a like number of militiamen. Tragedy seemed imminent. Thornwell ran to the scene and without hesitation plunged into the hotheaded students, urging calm. He said he would personally investigate their grievances. If they were right, and had no other recourse, he would return and lead the attack himself. The professor then began marching toward their campus shouting, "College! College!" To his great relief, the boys followed. He led them into the chapel where he talked for a time, further calming them and ending the crisis. Thornwell's heroism became the talk of the town.[57]

Heading off a student riot proved to be but one success amid a series of reverses and afflictions that would plague Thornwell during these years at the seminary. In addition to teaching, he had taken on the editorship of the *Southern Quarterly Review*, a well-respected but insufficiently supported journal of opinion. "In relation to the *Review*, I am sadly discouraged," he wrote to a friend. "The work has been warmly praised; but praises pay neither printer, editor, nor contributors." The periodical continued its decline and finally ceased publication.

The Brooks-Sumner Affair, and its aftermath, also left him depressed. Thornwell's congressman, Preston Brooks, thrashed Charles Sumner of Massachusetts at his Senate desk in retaliation for insulting remarks. Abolitionists lionized the battered Sumner while admirers from across the South sent new canes to Brooks with admonitions to "hit him again!" Thornwell felt only sadness. "The future is very dark. The North seems to be mad, and the South blind..."[58]

In the fall of 1856 a series of personal tragedies struck. Thornwell's mother came down with typhoid while visiting Columbia and died. Thornwell returned with her body to Bennettsville, South Carolina, reluctantly leaving two sick children at home. Eight-year-old son Witherspoon seemed to be coping with the illness better than his older sister. Named Nancy Witherspoon Thornwell, the seventeen year old had always been called "Nannie." Returning home from his mother's funeral, Thornwell met his wife at the front door. There was something very wrong.

"Tell me the worst," blurted out the anxious father, "tell me if my dear daughter is dead."

"No," was the tearful reply, "but Witherspoon is; he died about half an hour ago."

Thornwell collapsed in grief and had to be helped to his room. A month later he was able to tell a friend how he had "suffered, and suffered keenly, and suffered, as I hope never to suffer again," yet without rebelling against God. "The gospel which I have long believed, and preached because I believe, was a very present help in time of trouble."[59]

Though teaching young seminarians was his primary responsibility, Thornwell also co-pastored Columbia's Presbyterian Church. Each year he journeyed to the General Assembly, often extending the trip to build goodwill and raise financial backing for the seminary. At the 1859 assembly in Indianapolis he was taken aback to hear someone propose that the church endorse the colonization of blacks to Africa. The merits of the scheme did not concern him. Once again he must make them understand that "the church is exclusively a *spiritual* organization, and possesses only a *spiritual* power." As Christ's representative on earth she must never "mix up with any political party, or any issue aside from her direct mission." As he finished his extemporaneous remarks a rare ripple of applause swept the hall.

Thornwell returned directly to Columbia from Indianapolis. His oldest daughter Nannie, described as "bright and attractive," was engaged to be married to a young preacher and the ceremony was just days away. Invitations had already been mailed but much preparation remained.

On arriving home Thornwell was shocked to find that Nannie had been sick for two days with a raging fever. She rapidly became worse and the distraught father called in two more doctors. They gave little hope and Thornwell felt she must be told. "She was not at all disconcerted. She assured me that her peace was made with God." Each member of the family came to her bedside to say good-bye. Her father spent the next day praying with her, reading the Bible aloud and gently talking to her about life after death. "Before the last hour came," Thornwell recounted later, "she had a momentary conflict; but gained a glorious victory, and her joy was irrepressible. She threw her arms around my neck, and told me that her happiness was beyond expression."

Nannie, clad in her wedding dress, was buried in Columbia's Elmwood Cemetery. The words carved on her gravestone were inspired by the Revelation of St. John the Divine: "SHE DESCENDED TO THE GRAVE, ADORNED AS A BRIDE TO MEET THE BRIDEGROOM." Thornwell's faith remained as strong as ever. But a close friend noticed that he was not quite the same man, that "a tinge of sadness rested upon his countenance" and there remained.[60]

———

The Supreme Court of the United States delivered in the spring of 1857 a decision that left abolitionists, and even many of their political rivals, reeling in confusion. A slave from Missouri named Dred Scott had, over a period of years, accompanied his master to a free state and to territory declared free by the Missouri Compromise. Abolitionists thought they saw in Scott's experience an opportunity to challenge slavery in the courts. They contended that merely residing in free territory had permanently conferred freedom on their client. Scott's case got nowhere in Missouri's judicial system and lost in federal circuit court before being appealed to the United States Supreme Court. The result was a bombshell. Chief Justice Roger Taney ruled that Scott could not even sue in federal court because he was not a citizen. According to Taney, legal precedent and American tradition confirmed that no black, free or slave, could be "a citizen of the United States within the meaning of the Constitution." From the very beginning, wrote the chief justice, blacks were naturally "regarded as beings of an inferior order; and altogether unfit to associate with the white race, either in social or political relations; and so far inferior that they had no rights which the white man was bound to respect..." In restricting slavery the Missouri Compromise had infringed on property rights guaranteed by the Constitution, continued Taney. The compromise was void. Congress could not prohibit slavery in any territory of the United States.

The new Republican Party had been founded on the principle of congressional exclusion of slavery from the territories. Now the High Court had knocked their platform out from under them and left them groping for a response. Some pretended to believe that those words dealing with slavery in the territories were *obiter dictum* and not legally binding. A few found themselves arguing against judicial review itself, while Republican congressmen looked forward to the day they might pack the Court and overturn the decision. Southerners, of course, were delighted. But the decision created problems for Democratic candidates coveting presidential ambitions. To side with the Court might win nods of approval from Southerners, but prove to be political suicide elsewhere. Desperate to find a way out of the dilemma, Douglas theorized that slavery might still be excluded by the people of a territory if they simply enacted no slave code. It was hopeless. His hairsplitting, the "Freeport Doctrine," failed to keep antislavery Democrats in the fold and did nothing for the "Little Giant's" popularity in the South.[61]

If many Southerners thought Douglas too often pusillanimous, those they called "Black Republicans" were unspeakable. Former Illinois Congressman Abraham Lincoln, though professing to respect the constitutional right of states to retain slavery, in June 1858 made his famous "House Divided" speech. In it he claimed that both free and slave states could not permanently coexist within the Union. Lincoln and other Republicans pointed to the *Dred Scott* decision as evidence of a "slave power conspiracy," claiming that Southerners, aided by Northern Democrats, were plotting to make the United States entirely slave. Republican Senator William H. Seward went so far as to declare that an "irrepressible conflict" existed between North and South, a struggle that must end in total victory for one section or the other.

Conservatives in both sections remembered that a "house divided" had formed the Union, eight slave states joining with five that had but recently chosen to abandon the institution. Responding to the Republicans, Douglas declared himself "opposed to that whole system of sectional agitation, which can produce nothing but strife, but discord, but hostility, and, finally, disunion..." The Illinois senator placed the blame for trouble squarely on Northern abolitionists. "Why should this slavery agitation be kept up?" he asked Lincoln. "Why cannot we be content to administer this Government as it was made—a confederacy of sovereign and independent States?"[62]

Debating Lincoln served to expose Douglas's weaknesses as a national candidate. But the senator appealed to racial feeling to win the applause of

Illinois audiences and put Lincoln and some of his abolitionist supporters on the defensive. "I would not endanger the perpetuity of this Union," said Douglas. "I would not blot out the great inalienable rights of the white men for all the negroes that ever existed." In 1851 Indiana and Iowa had banned immigration to their states by any black, free or slave. Two years later Illinois citizens added the same provision to their constitution.

Lincoln was quick to distance himself from any egalitarian fringe element that might prove an embarrassment. It did not follow, he joked, that just "because I do not want a negro woman for a slave I must necessarily have her for a wife." Blacks had a right to "life, liberty and the pursuit of happiness," but with certain necessary restrictions. "I am not, nor ever have been in favor," said Lincoln, "of bringing about in any way the social and political equality of the white and black races..." Blacks must be free. But freed blacks, in Lincoln's view, must not be permitted to vote, serve on juries, hold office or, of course, mix with whites.[63]

———

Even as Douglas and Lincoln spoke, one band of antislavery zealots prepared for their version of Armageddon. John Brown—financed by prominent New England abolitionists impressed by his record of terrorism—stockpiled weapons, gathered recruits and laid his plans.

His appearance was that of a simple working man. Disheveled hair matched his unkempt clothes, his face etched with the cares of nearly sixty years. From downturned mouth to knitted brow, his countenance seemed frozen in a permanent scowl. But it was that piercing stare that people remembered. His eyes burned with hatred—hatred of slavery—hatred of racial inequality—and contempt for any who doubted his divine mission.

Restless, forever moving from place to place, Brown could never put down roots or stick with one job for long. But in the struggle against slavery he was unwavering. He served for a time as a "conductor" on the "underground railroad," lived in a black community in New York and taught former slaves in Pennsylvania. In 1855 Brown decided that his services were needed in the West. He and five of his sons moved to Kansas Territory, then a battleground between settlers and partisan outsiders on both sides of the slavery question. With cold-blooded efficiency the Browns descended one night on settlers at Pottawatomie, dragging five men away from their families into the darkness, hacking them to death with cold steel blades. Fleeing east, unmolested by the law, Brown gloried in his notoriety as he made new plans. All that came before had been prologue. The beast of slavery must now be slain in its lair.

In October 1859 Brown led a platoon of his white and black revolutionaries into western Virginia. They terrorized the citizens of Harpers Ferry, seized the federal arsenal there and waited for the slaves to rise up and join them in a massive revolt. None did. Ironically, the first victim of their shooting spree was a free black man. Brown's band was quickly surrounded in the arsenal by militiamen and assaulted the next day by a company of United States Marines under the command of an army colonel named Robert E. Lee. In minutes it was over. Wounded, under arrest, with half his men dead, Brown's plot seemed a total failure. He was tried by the state of Virginia, found guilty of treason and murder and promptly hanged.

When Southerners first heard of Brown's raid they were angry and apprehensive. A measure of calm returned when it became clear that slaves had ignored his appeals. Brown had embraced the role of martyr while in prison and at his trial. But conservatives, North and South, were unprepared for what happened next.

On the day of his execution church bells tolled across the North as millions mourned his passing. Abolitionist poets hailed him as a "saint" and "crucified hero" who would "make the gallows as glorious as the cross."[64] All this for a man who would see slavery drowned in the blood of women and children. Conservatives of all persuasions were shocked to the core. Never had extremism appeared so widespread or respectable. Southerners who had not flinched in their steadfast unionism now seemed to feel the very ground shift beneath their feet.

IV.

Charleston, that most Southern of cities, had never seen such an assembly as that which gathered at South Carolina Institute Hall on April 23 for the opening gavel of the 1860 Democratic National Convention. By steamship, stagecoach and rail car they came. From Minnesota to Mississippi, Maine to California, every state in the Union was represented. Some free-state men witnessed slavery, and a multiracial society, for the first time. Delegates thronged the streets of South Carolina's port city, surged through crowded hotel lobbies, sampled the cuisine and caucused behind closed doors.

All sides were girded for battle. If they could make Douglas the nominee Northern Democrats thought they just might halt the erosion of support that had plagued their party back home. The Little Giant badly wanted the nomination, but on a platform Northern voters could tolerate. Southern Democrats, on the other hand, refused to back down on their demand for protection of slavery in the territories. They argued that the institution might be regulated by statute or ultimately abolished, but was based in the common law and required no legislation to establish it. Once a territory achieved statehood its people then acquired the sovereign right to decide the future of slavery. In the meantime, since America's territories were the common property of all, simple equity demanded that the rights of slaveholders be respected. By protecting slavery in the territories Congress was making it possible for the people to choose freedom when statehood came. For Congress or a territorial legislature to exclude slavery only guaranteed the admission of another free state.

Common sense might dictate that slavery would never take root in the West anyway, that there was little likelihood of another slave state ever joining the Union. Yet many Southerners felt that the battle over the territories was part of a larger struggle, one in which they expected greater sympathy and understanding from their political allies of the Democratic Party. "What right of yours, gentlemen of the North," scolded William L. Yancey at the Charleston convention, "have we of the South ever invaded? What institution of yours have we ever assailed, directly or indirectly?" It was the South that had everything at stake in the slavery controversy. Even if Northerners were right about slavery in the territories they had little to lose, said Yancey, by yielding "as brothers, in order to quiet our doubts."

As a young newspaperman in Greenville, South Carolina Yancey had wielded his pen against Calhoun and nullification. After migrating to Alabama his political views shifted as he became a defender of states' rights in the legislature, United States Congress and as leader of the state's Democrats. Through his League of United Southerners Yancey beat the drum for secession and a Southern confederacy. But his greatest contribution to regional unity was the "Alabama Platform," a manifesto that called for, among other things, congressional protection of slavery in the territories and denial of any local authority to exclude the institution. Several state Democratic parties demanded the platform's adoption prior to the nomination of a candidate in Charleston. Should it fail, they pledged to walk out.

Most Southern delegates held back from threats of a walkout, but stood together on the issue of congressional protection of slavery in the territories. When the crucial vote came a majority of states, including even California and Oregon, backed the Southern position. But the delegate total fell short. True to their promise, most or all of the delegates from Alabama, Mississippi, Louisiana, Texas, Arkansas, Florida, Georgia and South Carolina walked out. Douglas supporters were unable to secure the two-thirds majority needed to nominate and the convention adjourned in frustration.[65] After much posturing and maneuvering Northern and Southern factions would later reconvene separately, Douglas to receive the nomination of his shattered party as Southern Democrats chose Kentucky's John C. Breckinridge as their champion.

———

To family and friends Thornwell said little as political clouds darkened the skies during the spring of 1860. Though his mind absorbed the import of events during these months, he chose to keep his own counsel and occupy himself with his Lord's work. In the wake of Nannie's death his thoughts dwelt on the spiritual welfare of his surviving children. Jane and Pattie were converted and "within the ark of safety." But in every letter to his boys he pressed the claims of the gospel. "My cup of earthly happiness would be full," he wrote to fifteen-year-old Gillespie, "if you, and

Jimmie, and Charlie, were only true Christians." Even the agitation and anxiety produced by John Brown's raid seemed not to affect Thornwell. In the midst of the excitement he departed Columbia for Mobile, Alabama on a fund-raising trip for the seminary. Yet when tubercular symptoms flared up he decided it would be wise to flee the unmerciful heat and humidity of the approaching Carolina summer. Two decades earlier a season in Europe had done much to restore his strength and Thornwell made plans to return.

In May 1860, even as Democrats reeled from the Charleston debacle, Thornwell journeyed to Rochester, New York for the Presbyterians' annual meeting. He was much involved in the proceedings, preached twice and reported to his wife that fellow church members "have been very kind and hospitable."[66] When the assembly adjourned he made for New York City and on June 2 boarded the steamship *Adriatic* for the ten-day voyage to England. Accompanying him this time was his daughter Jane, her preacher husband and several friends.

Docking at Southhampton, they spent a few weeks touring the British Isles. In London Thornwell enjoyed Westminster Abbey, the Tower, the British Museum and rows of dusty shops stacked high with used books. His party meandered through France, Belgium, the Germanic Confederation and Switzerland, where Calvin's Geneva most captured Thornwell's imagination. Still, he could not help but remain the proud and patriotic American. "I could keep you up night after night with the wonders I have seen," he told Nancy. "But my native land is dearer than ever." News of deepening division at home troubled his mind. He prayed that his countrymen might yet "have the grace to deal justly and honourably with one another, and to hold together as a people." He wrestled with the problem. Perhaps if the South could make some move in the direction of emancipation the sectional agitation would cease. Almost anything seemed worth the effort.[67] Was there some way to avoid disunion, or had division by now become inevitable?

Returning to South Carolina in September, after an absence of some four months, Thornwell found America in the midst of its most polarizing election campaign. Republicans had met in May, nominated the ticket of Lincoln and Hannibal Hamlin, and adopted a carefully-worded platform. States' rights were paid lip service, though talk of secession they denounced as "contemplated treason." The Supreme Court's decision in *Dred Scott* was repudiated as "a dangerous political heresy."[68] Lincoln, some admitted, was not the most objectionable candidate they could have put forward. But to Southerners the nominee mattered little. The Republican Party itself had become abolitionism's political vehicle, promoter of "irrepressible conflict" with the South, led by revolutionaries who would twist the Constitution to their own purposes. Republican opposition to slavery in the territories was suspected by many to be but a preliminary step in a campaign to overthrow slavery everywhere. Capture of the White House by "Black Republicans" would place the power of the presidency in the hands of zealots determined to make the South their victim and the federal government their weapon. South Carolina newspaper editors and political leaders of nearly every persuasion demanded some form of resistance should Lincoln win. To most, that meant secession.

Alone among the states in 1860, South Carolina held no election for president, the state's eight electors chosen by vote of the General Assembly. Not that it mattered. The Palmetto State was nearly unanimous in support of Breckinridge, thirty-nine-year-old vice president of the United States, and his running mate, Senator Joseph Lane of Oregon. They stood without apology for federal protection of slavery in the territories and enforcement of the Fugitive Slave Law.

Douglas Democrats attempted to ignore party divisions by adopting a platform that merely promised obedience to High Court decisions. Nominating former Georgia Governor Herschel Johnson for vice president might also, thought Douglas supporters, tempt Southerners to return to the fold. Further dividing Lincoln's opposition was a "fourth party" backing former Tennessee Senator John Bell for president and Edward Everett of Massachusetts for vice president. Calling themselves the Constitutional Union Party, they earnestly if naively pledged to support "the Constitution...the Union...and the enforcement of the laws."[69]

Election day came and Douglas's support in the South turned out to be negligible, though he took Missouri by a narrow plurality. Bell was able to carry Tennessee, Kentucky and Virginia. Breckinridge and Lane captured the remaining eleven Dixie states. Lincoln received no votes at all in two-thirds of the Southern states, his best showing a third-place finish in little Delaware. Yet despite thirty-nine percent popular support nationally, Lincoln's electoral college majority was insurmountable. Every free state except New Jersey was in his column. He received votes from a Northern coalition that included everyone from egalitarian abolitionists to those who felt that only Republicans, as the "White Man's Party," could keep blacks out of the territories. Though done in a perfectly legal fashion, a sectional candidate— backed by a minority of Americans—had captured the reins of government. All sides recognized it as a radical departure. "The great revolution," exulted Massachusetts Republican Charles Francis Adams, "has actually taken place."[70]

———

On election day South Carolina lawmakers chose electors pledged to Breckinridge and Lane, then voted to remain in session until the telegraph could flash news of the outcome. It was assumed by South Carolinians that a Lincoln victory would be followed by secession. Through the summer and fall new battle lines had formed within the state over how leaving the

Union might actually be accomplished. Advocates of separate state secession insisted that action by South Carolina would embolden other states to follow. Should the North dare to attempt interference, the whole South would rush to the defense of the seceded states. Separate state actionists had confidence in their scenario, but insisted that the Palmetto State secede with or without promises of help. After all, they pointed out, each state is sovereign and must act independently. Cooperationists, on the other hand, were pledged to secession — but in concert with other states. Some of them spoke of cooperative action by a Southern convention, others proposed simultaneous secession by a block of states, anything to avoid South Carolina's isolation. As election day approached and it became clear that at least some other states would follow South Carolina's lead, the cooperationists' cautious position became less tenable. There was also a small but respected minority of unionists in the state. Centered around Greenville and led by newspaperman Benjamin F. Perry, their unionism was conditioned on the Lincoln administration committing no act of aggression. They made it equally clear that they would remain loyal to South Carolina in whatever course the state followed. True unionism, a willingness to submit unconditionally to federal authority, was virtually non-existent in South Carolina.[71]

The South's dilemma was not without sympathy in the North. Just after the election the New York *Herald* blamed years of antislavery agitation for first splitting the churches and then dividing the political parties. In sectionalism's triumph "we shall find good reason why the South should be in earnest in its present alarm." Douglas Democrats, supported by leaders from the Upper South, scrambled to come up with compromise measures and constitutional amendments that might calm the Deep South and head off secession. Each proposal was blocked by congressional Republicans. "Compromise - Compromise! why I am sick at the very idea," wrote William Herndon, Lincoln's law partner, to Senator Charles Sumner. "I am thoroughly convinced that two such civilizations as the North and South cannot co-exist on the same soil and be co-equal in the Federal brotherhood...Let this natural war — let this inevitable struggle proceed — go on, till slavery is *dead - dead - dead*."[72]

South Carolina's reaction to Lincoln's victory was swift. On November 10 the General Assembly enacted legislation providing for an election in four weeks to choose convention delegates. This convention of the people would meet on December 17 to decide South Carolina's future. There had already been extensive communication among Southern political leaders prior to Lincoln's election. Now commissioners from other states of the Lower South officially urged secession, promising that their own people would follow.

Carolinians were not waiting on a convention to make their feelings known. Daily they declared their independence, caught up in a movement that gathered momentum and carried all before it. In Charleston Judge

Andrew G. Magrath of the United States District Court stood in his court-room, pulled off his black robe and publicly resigned, lest under Lincoln his court be "desecrated with sacrifices to tyranny." The district attorney and other federal officers soon joined him. The state's senators left Washington, followed by the House delegation. Blue secession cockades became the rage in South Carolina as palmetto flags of all sizes, colors and descriptions blossomed everywhere. Twenty thousand cheering Charlestonians rallied for secession, erecting a liberty pole at the corner of Meeting and Hayne Streets. In every town and village militia companies drilled, cannon boomed, bands played and orators cried for action. Robert Barnwell Rhett felt vindicated at last. Old political divisions were disappearing. "No Black Republican President," thundered the once-moderate James L. Orr of Anderson, "should ever execute any law within our borders unless at the point of a bayonet and over the dead bodies of our slain sons." Charleston unionist Michael O'Connor declared for secession, Lincoln's Union now "a dead carcass stinking in the nostrils of the Southern people." Francis Pickens, South Carolina politician and recently the United States ambassador to Russia, demanded "Independence, now and *forever*." Congressman Lawrence Keitt of Orangeburg District exhorted a crowd in Columbia to "unfurl the flag and, with the sword of State, cut the bonds of this accursed Union."[73]

———

South Carolina legislators had called for "a day of fasting, humiliation and prayer" to be observed on Wednesday, November 21 and all around the Palmetto State the faithful gathered in their places of worship. From the pulpit of Columbia's Presbyterian Church James Henley Thornwell gazed across the congregation. Perhaps his mind wandered back to his youth when he had rejected Dr. Cooper's teachings to oppose nullification. For nearly three decades Thornwell had resisted the rising secessionist tide. Though the Union was about to be swept away, he could take satisfaction in knowing that through his efforts Presbyterians held together as a national denomination. Now, even as pressure for secession continued to build, fellow church members came to hear his thoughts on the meaning of Lincoln's triumph at the polls. He titled his sermon "Our National Sins."

Thornwell felt that it was not his place "to plead the cause of States' rights or Federal authority," despite the gravity of the situation. "During the twenty five years in which I have fulfilled my course as a preacher—all of which have been spent in my native State, and nearly all in this city—I have never introduced secular politics into the instructions of the pulpit." Though he would not as a clergyman recommend a course of action, neither could he as a citizen remain silent. The Union he had loved was at the point of death. Thornwell accepted the fact that South Carolina's secession was the manifest will of the people and by now irresistible. Under the circumstances he felt that to comment from the pulpit would not be inconsistent with his long-standing concern for "the spirituality of the church."

He began by reviewing America's history as he and his hearers understood it. They all agreed that the states emerged from the revolutionary war with their independence intact. By voluntarily joining together they had achieved unity while preserving their diversity. Under the Constitution state sovereignty had not been surrendered. "The laws of Congress bind me, only because South Carolina has consented that I should be bound," said Thornwell. "The rights of Congress are only the concessions of the sovereign States." By necessity such an arrangement "depends upon a scrupulous adherence to good faith." But Northern states had proven themselves treacherous by denying the right of slaveholders to go into the territories and by refusing to abide by the Fugitive Slave Law. Abolitionists had shattered his hopes for American greatness. "It was ours to redeem this continent," said Thornwell, with perhaps some bitterness. "We were a city set upon a hill, whose light was intended to shine upon every people and upon every land." Both North and South had been too much inclined to pride and sectional prejudice. But the North, he said, was guilty of far greater sin by breaking the compact.

Thornwell once again denounced as the "offspring of infidelity" any speculation that questioned "the common brotherhood" of humanity. Slave and master have "the same Father, the same Redeemer, and the same everlasting destiny." But the fatherhood of God did not for Thornwell mean that the races were equally endowed. Nor did the brotherhood of man require an enforced equality of condition. "Let us apply with unflinching candour the golden rule of our Savior," said Thornwell. "Have we rendered to our slaves what, if we were in their circumstances, we should think it right and just in them to render to us? We are not bound to render unto them what they may in fact desire. Such a rule would transmute morality into arbitrary caprice. But we are bound to render unto them what they have a right to desire..."

He warned South Carolinians of hardships to come. This was not the kind of message they had been hearing. On every hand politicians were predicting an easy, perhaps bloodless, victory in the event secession was resisted. Thornwell had no such illusions. "Even though our cause be just, and our course approved by heaven, our path to victory may be through a baptism of blood." And no sacrifice, however great, could guarantee South Carolina's triumph. Still, "It will not follow, even if she should be destined to fall, that her course was wrong, or her suffering in vain."[74]

The election for convention delegates proceeded quietly and produced a body Thornwell later described as "sober, grave, and venerable." Conservatives were chosen along with long-time secessionists such as Rhett. This cross section of the state's most mature political leadership gathered at noon on December 17 for their first session at the new sanctuary of Columbia's Baptist Church. Concerned about reports of smallpox in the city, the convention adjourned at ten that night to re-convene in Charleston the next afternoon. Organizational details behind them, on December 20 delegates took their seats in the hall of the St. Andrew's Society on Broad Street, ready at last to take the action for which they had been elected.

The Ionic-columned structure was old but handsome. To the right towered the Catholic cathedral and on the left stood the century-old home of John Rutledge, leader of the state during revolutionary days. The business at hand was simple enough. On the table lay a document that would repeal the 1788 ordinance that ratified the United States Constitution. It declared "that the union now subsisting between South Carolina and other States under the name the United States of America is hereby dissolved." One by one, in alphabetical order, the vote was recorded. From James Hopkins Adams to Henry C. Young, all 169 delegates voted "aye."[75]

Across the city shops and businesses had closed their doors and a multitude stood in Broad Street, awaiting the outcome. At 1:15 P.M. came the shouted report. The news spread like a roaring wave through the crowd and across the city, to be taken up by telegraph operators and flashed throughout the land. "THE UNION IS DISSOLVED!" screamed a *Mercury* "extra." Celebrations continued all afternoon. Near dusk the delegates formed in procession, marched east down Broad and turned left onto Meeting Street beneath the steeple of St. Michael's Church. Windows and balconies along the route were festooned with a profusion of flags and banners bearing the devices of defiant sovereignty. The parade passed the fireproof Records Building, Hibernian Hall and the five-story Mills House Hotel with its dozens of glowing windows. At South Carolina Institute Hall delegates paused, then filed through the front doors of the great building.

Charleston's largest meeting place, described as "Venetian" in architectural style, the hall had been chosen for the ceremonial signing of the Ordinance of Secession. Newly-elected Governor Francis Pickens, the General Assembly and some three thousand others witnessed as delegates came forward to affix their signatures. That done, convention President David F. Jamison stood to speak. "The Ordinance of Secession has been signed and ratified," he solemnly announced, "and I proclaim the State of South Carolina an Independent Commonwealth." Thunderous applause rocked the hall. Outside the December night was illuminated with bonfires, Roman candles and bursting rockets. To the thud of exploding fireworks was added a cacophony of pealing church bells, cannon salutes, martial music and shouting crowds. All through the night the delirious demonstration went on.

Across the dark harbor lay Sullivan's Island, surrounded by moonlit beach and pungent marshland. On the southern end of the barrier island stood the weathered brick walls of Fort Moultrie, commanded by Major Robert Anderson of the United States Army. From atop the parapet this night he could, in the distance, witness his country's dissolution.

It was said that on Secession Day the most serene place in the city of Charleston was the hall where the convention sat. It had been over thirty-five years since Cooper issued his challenge that fellow citizens "calculate the value of the Union." Twenty-eight years had passed since South Carolina nearly went to war with President Jackson over nullification. At mid-century the state had marched again to the brink of secession only to pull back. Now delegates representing every political current within the state were united in their resolve. They had been deliberate, unafraid, supremely confident of being in the right. "Whatever else may be said of it," wrote Thornwell, "it certainly must be admitted that the solemn act of South Carolina was well considered."

Thornwell laid out his views in an article published in the *Southern Presbyterian Review* just after South Carolina acted. In it he insisted that secession of his state was not triggered by grievances over the tariff or hope of economic gain. Disunionism could only "have mustered a corporal's guard" if based on nothing more than a desire for free trade. "The real cause of the intense excitement of the South," he continued, "is the profound conviction that the Constitution, in its relation to slavery, has been virtually repealed; that the Government has assumed a new and dangerous attitude upon the subject; that we have, in short, new terms of union submitted to our acceptance or rejection. Here lies the evil. The election of Lincoln, when properly interpreted, is nothing more nor less than a proposition to the South to consent to a Government, fundamentally different upon the question of slavery, from that which our fathers established."

South Carolina's response to Lincoln was therefore not against him personally, but was based on what he represented. "His election seals the triumph of those principles, and that triumph seals the subversion of the Constitution, in relation to a matter of paramount interest to the South." Equality between the sections, the neutrality of the federal government regarding slavery — had these fundamentals been in doubt the Southern states would never have ratified the Constitution. As opinion elsewhere changed over the years, Southerners found no reason to abandon the traditional view of slavery. "From the first dawn of authentic history, until the present period, it has come down to us through all the course of ages," said Thornwell. Yet the election of Lincoln establishes for the first time the federal government's hostility toward the institution. From now on things will be different. "The North becomes the United States, and the South a subject province."

It was more than an election that had been lost, insisted Thornwell. "This is a thorough and radical revolution. It makes a new Government; it proposes new and extraordinary terms of union. The old Government is as completely abolished as if the people of the United States had met in convention and repealed the Constitution. It is frivolous to tell us that the change has been made through the forms of the Constitution. This is to add insult to injury. What signify forms, when the substance is gone?" The revolution would begin in earnest with Lincoln's inauguration. "The oath which makes him President, makes a new Union. The import of secession is simply the refusal, on the part of the South, to be parties to any such Union."

Withdrawal from the United States was not taken lightly by most South Carolinians. "It was a painful struggle to ourselves; the most painful of our lives,"said Thornwell, and he understood the hesitation of other Southern states. But a new confederacy, made up of those with common interests, would be strong enough to survive in a hostile world. Secession did not signify the failure of America's experiment in freedom and self-government. Two Unions "may work out the problems of human liberty more successfully than one," even as they "save this continent for republicanism for ever."

Every attempt at compromise within the Union had failed, said Thornwell, because of a Northern attitude that permitted only "complete surrender, on one side or the other." Now he prayed for an amicable separation. "We prefer peace," he concluded, "but if war must come, we are prepared to meet it with unshaken confidence in the God of battles."[76]

Virginia looks on for the present with her arms folded, but she only bides her time.

John Tyler[1]

Forlorn Hope of Compromise
John Tyler

The news from South Carolina electrified secessionists across the Cotton States.

Mississippi's convention convened on January 7, 1861 and two days later, by a vote of 84 to 15, took the Magnolia State out of the Union. The only opposition to secession had come from the hill counties in the northeastern part of the state. As a symbol of their independence a large blue flag emblazoned with a white star was hoisted above the Mississippi capitol, a sight that inspired song writer Harry Macarthy to compose "The Bonnie Blue Flag."

Down in Florida there were pockets of unionism near Jacksonville and a few cautious Floridians were initially concerned that secession might leave the state isolated. But the sobering reality of Lincoln's election swept away all doubts. On January 10 the state convention in Tallahassee approved an Ordinance of Secession 62 to 7.

The very next day Alabama seceded by a vote of 61 to 39. True unionism was hardly an issue. Many of the "no" votes came from cooperationists still desiring "consultation" with other states prior to taking action. A resolution rejecting Lincoln's authority in Alabama had already passed the convention by a unanimous vote. Alabama's secession created a contiguous block of three independent states separated from South Carolina only by Georgia.

In Georgia, second-largest state east of the Mississippi River, secession had for months been the subject of intensive debate. Prominent unionists

John Tyler

such as Alexander H. Stephens and Herschel V. Johnson urged a wait-and-see attitude toward the incoming administration. But the secessionist tide proved irresistible. On January 19 the Georgia convention voted 208 to 89 for independence, and most unionists rallied loyally to their state.

Louisiana had perhaps less sentiment for secession and more ties to the North than any other state of the Deep South. For months a spirited exchange had gone on between immediate secessionists, cooperationists and conditional unionists, but the momentum for secession steadily increased, especially after South Carolina stepped out. On January 26 the Louisiana convention voted 113 to 17 for secession. After registering their negative votes, ten of the antisecession delegates went ahead and signed their names to the ordinance.

Across the Sabine River in Texas the overwhelming majority were for abandoning Lincoln's Union, despite Governor Sam Houston's opposition. The Texas convention, meeting in Austin, voted on January 29 for independence by a vote of 152 to 6, subject to a referendum. A month later the people confirmed the decision with a seventy-six percent "yes" vote.[2]

Counted together, convention delegates in the seven states of the Deep South had voted for secession by a nearly five-to-one margin. Significant too was the fact that most of the "no" votes were cast by men with no thought of betraying their state in a conflict with federal authority.

That long-dreamed-of Southern confederacy was about to take form. Even before the state seceded, members of the South Carolina convention suggested a meeting for the purpose of forming a new republic. They finally proposed that representatives from the Southern states convene in Montgomery, Alabama on February 4, 1861. Most secessionists recognized the wisdom of having their own government in place prior to Lincoln taking office. Delegates from the seceded states were dispatched to Montgomery and there they set to work forming a provisional government and making a permanent new constitution.

That document would bear a striking resemblance to the Constitution of the United States. The Bill of Rights and other amendments were incorporated into the text, there was no ban on the admission of free states and re-opening the slave trade was prohibited. There were important reforms too. The president would be elected to a single term of six years, given a line-item veto, and his cabinet heads could take part in congressional debate. The Preamble made it clear that sovereignty resided in the people—not in the aggregate—but organized as sovereign states. And unlike the Constitution of 1787 that of the Confederate States of America began with an unapologetic invocation of "the favor and guidance of Almighty God."[3]

Still, the Upper South held back. The loss of an election was not sufficient cause to break up the Union, most insisted. There would first have to be some overt act of aggression on the part of the new administration. Opinion in the Volunteer State was typical. "Tennessee is emphatically a Union State if the Union can be preserved upon terms of equality and justice," explained the Nashville *Republican Banner*, "and is for making an attempt to preserve it before abandoning the hope." In a vote February 9 the people of Tennessee refused even to call a convention. Virginia and Missouri did elect delegates, but most opposed secession. Arkansas's sovereignty convention met in Little Rock and the unionist majority promptly voted to adjourn. North Carolinians narrowly rejected the calling of a convention, many of the "yes" votes in the referendum cast by unionists confident of controlling the body once it met. Kentuckians, deeply divided, prayed for some eleventh-hour compromise. There was secessionist sentiment in the Maryland legislature but stalwart unionist Governor Thomas Hicks refused to convene the lawmakers. In Delaware the legislature condemned secession even as Governor William Burton, sympathetic to the South, pleaded for accommodation. Though immediate prospects for adding new states seemed dim, Confederates were encouraged when the legislatures of Virginia and Missouri passed resolutions in January warning against federal use of force.[4]

Disunion had unexpected ramifications. Consumers in the seceded states were canceling orders made with Northern businesses, some even repudiating debts. Committees demanding compromise with the South were formed by bankers and merchants in Boston and New York City. Mayor Fernando Wood delivered a message to the New York City Common Council on January 6 declaring the breakup of the country to be inevitable. New Yorkers, he insisted, "have friendly relations and a common sympathy" with the South. "We have not participated," he said, "in the warfare upon their constitutional rights..." Now that the United States was going to pieces he recommended that New Yorkers, one million strong, look to their own interests as an independent city-state. New Jersey was also restive. And there was talk of California and Oregon forming an independent republic on the west coast.[5]

Former President of the United States John Tyler was deeply disturbed at what he saw happening to the country. Almost seventy-one years old, in declining health, the aristocratic Virginian kept up with events from "Sherwood Forest," his plantation home on the James River. He expressed astonishment at the "lunacy which seems to have seized the North," in their embracing of Lincoln and his revolutionary designs. "What imaginable good is to come to them," he wondered, "by compelling the Southern States into secession?" Fellow Southerners were partly to blame, to be sure. The walkout at the Charleston Democratic Convention had been a mistake, believed the ex-president, contributing as it did to the shattering of the party. Prior to the breakup in Charleston, Tyler had himself been mentioned as a "dark horse" presidential candidate. Afterwards he urged a fusion of the Bell and Douglas forces and the withdrawal of Breckinridge, if all factions would agree to make a united front against Lincoln. When that failed he backed Breckinridge in the hope that no candidate would receive a majority of electoral college votes, allowing the House of Representatives to decide. He reasoned that a congressional compromise might put Oregon's reliable Joseph Lane in the White House. From the opening of the campaign a Republican victory had been to Tyler a thing of dread. "I fear that we have fallen on evil times," he wrote soon after Lincoln's triumph, "and that the day of doom for the great model republic is at hand."[6]

"Tippecanoe and Tyler too!" was the lilting slogan of the Whig Party in the 1840 campaign. Twenty-nine years earlier William Henry Harrison had routed the Shawnee at Tippecanoe in the Indiana Territory and party strategists jumped at the chance to exploit whatever image he retained as a military hero. Tyler, as an independent-minded Democrat, seemed an excellent choice to balance the ticket.

Tyler's political career began with his election, at age twenty-one, to the Virginia legislature. The son of a governor, he had studied at William and Mary and been admitted to the bar while still in his teens. Two terms in the United States House of Representatives were followed by his own election to the governorship. Along the way he found time to play the violin, compose a little romantic verse and marry the beautiful and gentle Letitia Christian.

In 1827 Governor Tyler was nominated for the United States senate seat held by the aging Randolph of Roanoke. Many in the General Assembly, though backers of Randolph's principles, had become concerned about the old man's eccentricities. Their votes, combined with about thirty cool to Randolph's stand on states' rights, would be enough to insure his defeat. Tyler needed that "federalist" block to win, but made a statement before the vote was taken deliberately distancing himself from their views. "My political opinions on the fundamental principles of Government," cautioned Tyler, "are the same as those espoused by Mr. Randolph, and I admire him most highly...and if any man votes for me under a different persuasion, he most grievously deceives himself." Tyler emerged the victor by a vote of 115 to 110. The incumbent representing Randolph's old district declined to run for re-election, instead endorsing Randolph's return to Congress. Revered by the people, Randolph would be elected to the lower house without opposition.[7]

Senator Tyler furthered his reputation as a strict constructionist, opposing protective tariffs, federally-funded internal improvements and the Missouri Compromise. State secession he upheld as a reserved right, though he could not accept the legality of nullification. After the Southern walkout he remained to cast the lone vote in the Senate against Jackson's Force Bill. Breaking with Jackson and the Democratic Party, in 1836 Tyler was a Whig nominee for vice president in a multi-candidate scheme that succeeded in throwing the election into the Senate. Although he lost there, he had captured the electoral votes of South Carolina, Maryland, Tennessee and Georgia. Four years later the Harrison-Tyler ticket carried nineteen of twenty-six states, routing the incumbent Democrat Martin Van Buren.

Harrison took the presidential oath of office in Washington on a bitterly cold day in March 1841. The sixty-eight year old then read a forgetable two-hour inaugural address to a crowd shivering in the bone-chilling wind and rain. The president came down with a persistent cold, the cold became pneumonia and on April 4 he was dead. Vice President Tyler was in Williamsburg when he received word that he was now the tenth president of the United States.

Or was he? No American president had ever died in office. A few sneeringly referred to Tyler as "His Accidency." Some insisted he consider himself merely "Acting President," a notion popular with Whig Party leaders who expected to control the former Democrat. Quickly Tyler made it clear he was chief executive in every sense of the word and the puppet of no one. He vetoed as unconstitutional two bills for a national bank sent to him by the Whig-controlled Congress. Within months his entire cabinet, except for Secretary of State Daniel Webster, had resigned and Tyler was expelled from his own party. Veto of a higher tariff led to an abortive attempt at impeachment. There were death threats and mobs burned him in effigy. A vindictive Congress even failed to appropriate funds for White House maintenance, forcing the president to pay utility bills himself.[8]

In the midst of his political troubles Letitia died, a stroke victim. The grieving president busied himself with his work. He was assisted in his White House social duties by his daughter Priscilla, under the occasional guidance of Dolley Madison. But Tyler would not remain single. Only four months after becoming a widower he began a most unlikely courtship.

Julia Gardiner, beautiful daughter of New York Senator David Gardiner, had visited at the White House with her family during the 1842–43 social season. The twenty-two-year-old Julia had a circle of admirers, and she soon added John Tyler to the list. They both had been below deck on the *Princeton* when Julia's father and so many others were killed in that tragic gun accident.

"Let me go to my father!" she shouted, struggling toward the upper deck in the aftermath of the explosion.

"My dear child, you can do no good," replied one who had witnessed the carnage above. "Your father is in heaven."

Julia fainted. When boats came alongside to take off the survivors, President Tyler himself carried her to safety.

Julia was actually five years younger than the president's oldest daughter. Her relationship with Tyler developed quickly. He was overwhelmed by his good fortune in winning Julia's heart, though not unmindful of their thirty-year-age difference. He sought the advice of friend Henry Wise, and was cautioned that Julia just might be smitten by the office Tyler held more than by the middle-aged Virginian himself.

Tyler's pride was hurt. "Why, my dear sir, I am just full in my prime!"

Wise answered with a story about another old Virginia planter of his acquaintance who had set out to marry a young woman. The planter went to one of his servants, a friend and confidant named Toney, for advice.

"Massa," he replied, "you think you can stand dat?"

"Yes, Toney, why not? I am yet strong, and I can now, as well as ever I could, make her happy."

"Yes; but Massa," said Toney, "*you* is now in *your* prime, dat's true; but when she is in *her* prime, where den, Massa, will *your* prime be?"

Any reservations John Tyler and Julia Gardiner may have had were forgotten. In order to avoid unwanted publicity a quiet wedding secretly took place in New York in June 1844, an announcement made only after the ceremony. From all accounts the marriage was a happy one. The new Mrs. Tyler delighted in her role as the president's lady. "John Tyler is no fool," concluded a New York reporter, "and his selection of a bride clenches our assertions."[9]

On the defensive through much of his presidency, Tyler fared best in foreign affairs. Foremost was his work for the annexation of the Republic of Texas. He also settled a Maine boundary dispute with Canada, extended the Monroe Doctrine to Hawaii and signed America's first trade agreement with China. A treaty with Britain had the United States Navy patrol the African coast to intercept illegal slave ships. But Tyler, the president without a party, chose not to attempt a third-party re-election bid. He ended up backing James Knox Polk because the Democrat favored the consummation of Tyler's labor for Texas statehood.

After leaving office the former president was content to retire to Sherwood Forest, there to enjoy his children, struggle with bills, hunt deer and entertain guests. His mother-in-law was amused to once come upon him playing his fiddle "for the little children black and white to dance," he having as much fun as they. "I never saw a happier temperament than he possesses."[10] Still, America's growing sectional troubles played on his mind.

Held in esteem by a wide circle of friends and acquaintances North and South, Tyler was determined to use his influence to preserve the Union as he understood it and to avoid war. "The conqueror will walk at every step over smoldering ashes and beneath crumbling columns," should such a catastrophe occur. "States once proud and independent will no longer exist and the glory of the Union will have departed forever...The picture is too horrible and revolting to be dwelt upon." In a letter published January 17, 1861 in the Richmond *Enquirer* he called for an extraordinary convention to meet and work out a plan for compromise. Tyler's hope was that a body made up of representatives from the Border States would meet, hammer out an agreement, and present it to the rest of the country. Two days after his letter appeared the Virginia General Assembly passed a joint resolution asking for such a meeting to be held in Washington on February 4, but inviting all the states.[11]

A basis of settlement was assumed by most to be something like the Crittenden Compromise. A month earlier Kentucky Senator John J. Crittenden had proposed a series of constitutional amendments that would ban slavery in territory north of the line of the old Missouri Compromise, permitting the institution in territory to the south. Other Crittenden amendments dealt with such sensitive issues as protecting slavery in the District of Columbia and compensating owners for runaways harbored in Northern states. When President-elect Lincoln made it clear he would not tolerate a concession that left slavery in any portion of the territories the amendments were doomed. Crittenden responded with one more fervent appeal, citing the popular groundswell of support he said he was receiving. It was useless. For Republicans to countenance compromise would be, they felt, to admit that Southerners had been wronged in the past and had cause for alarm over the future. Besides, most thought further secession unlikely. On January 16 the United States Senate voted against Crittenden's amendments 25 to 23.

Republican refusal to compromise was based in part on their misunderstanding of Southern unionism. Some seemed hopelessly deluded. "I have believed firmly," said William H. Seward, "that everywhere, even in South Carolina, devotion to the Union is a profound and permanent national sentiment..." Seward would have had trouble finding many in the Deep South who might agree with his assessment. In those seven states secession had already swept across the political landscape like an avalanche, obliterating the old landmarks, the new scene unrecognizable. For the foreseeable future no compromise could bring back the seceded states. One visitor to Charleston in March would report that "separate nationality is a fixed fact...there is no attachment to the Union...The sentiment of national patriotism, always feeble in Carolina, has been extinguished and overridden by the acknowledged doctrine of the paramount allegiance to the State."

Even among opponents of secession in the Upper South there were few that Republicans would recognize as fellow unionists, willing to conform unconditionally to federal authority. Nor did Northerners seem to comprehend Southern adherence to what they called "principles." On January 25 the Charlottesville *Review*, one of Virginia's eloquent voices against secession, put the matter in perspective. "There is a habit of speaking derisively of going to war for an *idea* – an abstraction – something which you cannot see. This is precisely the point on which we would go to war...The people who will not fight for ideas will never retain the spirit to fight for anything. Life looses its highest meaning, when opinions become matters of indifference...Therefore, we say, for this *idea* of State honor – for this abstract principle of not bating her just claims upon threat of coercion – we would convulse this Union from centre to circumference."[12]

It was not only Republicans who misjudged the situation. Even the most well-intentioned advocates of compromise faced an impossible challenge.

Tyler was one of those who clung to the hope that it was not too late — that Republicans might moderate their demands and the Deep South be willing to rejoin a reconstructed Union. To pursue this goal he would have preferred a smaller, more manageable conference made up of Border States alone — six free and six slave. But the Virginia legislature invited all, and since the seceded states would of course send no delegates, the North would by default dominate the gathering. When the first session was called to order at the meeting hall of Willard's Hotel on February 4 eleven states were represented. That number soon grew to twenty one, seven slave and fourteen free. Some of the delegates were appointed by state legislatures and some by governors. But it was a distinguished body. Besides ex-President Tyler were six former cabinet members, nineteen who had been governors, fourteen ex-senators, fifty former congressmen and several who had served as ambassadors and judges. David Wilmot was there, now a "Black Republican." New Jersey delegate Robert Stockton, retired naval officer, had been captain of the *Princeton* that fateful day in 1844.[13]

Tyler had also been dispatched on a mission of peace to President James Buchanan. The men held two long meetings, Tyler urging the president to avoid "all acts calculated to produce a collision of arms" between the seceded states and federal authorities. Buchanan complained of federal property being seized after secession, but agreed that for now no hostile or retaliatory action would be taken. At one point Tyler recommended that federal troops be removed from Fort Sumter, leaving only a token force. If he did such a thing, replied Buchanan, he would be burned in effigy all across the North. "What of that, Sir?" answered Tyler. At times during his presidency he had been burned in effigy all across the land, the flames visible through the very windows of the White House. "But the light of those fires," he insisted, "enabled me only the more clearly to pursue the path of duty."[14] President Buchanan denied the right of secession, but neither could he bring himself to conclude that the federal government possessed the lawful authority to coerce a state. Tyler would have to be satisfied with that.

After a brief rest at home President and Mrs. Tyler returned to the capital for the convention. Julia was in her element. Headquartered at Brown's Hotel, she thoroughly enjoyed being again in the midst of Washington society. Not since her days as America's youngest First Lady had she been the object of so much attention. Proud she was too of her husband's prominence. "They are all looking to him in the settlement of the vexed question. His superiority over everybody else is felt and admitted by all."

Tyler went to Washington searching for, in his words, "that true glory" which saving the Union and avoiding war would bring. On the second day of the convention he was unanimously elected its president. In his speech of acceptance Tyler handsomely praised the states that had sent representatives for one last attempt at compromise. But he quickly discovered that the task was even more formidable than he imagined. Debate at times became so disorderly that he lost control. Most disturbing, he faced insurmountable intransigence on the part of the Republicans. Even as they appointed delegates the legislatures of Ohio, Illinois and Pennsylvania announced that they saw no need for constitutional amendments. Many Republicans were willing to talk only as a way of buying time, maintaining the status quo until Lincoln could take office. Michigan, Wisconsin and Minnesota refused to participate at all.[15]

Southern delegates insisted that there must be at least a theoretical possibility of slavery's expansion into some portion of the territories. Without this concession they were sure that luring seceded states back to the Union would be impossible. Republicans dug in their heels. To back down now would be to betray their party platform. Regardless of what the convention might agree to, no constitutional amendment that allowed slavery in even a portion of the territories had a chance of approval in the Republican-controlled state legislatures.

Considering the obstacles, it was perhaps surprising that delegates accomplished anything. The plan that emerged resembled Crittenden's, with a few modifications. Under the convention's proposed thirteenth amendment slavery would be prohibited north of the 36°30' line—effectively banning the institution forever from eighty percent of America's western lands. Overruling *Dred Scott*, slavery would be tolerated only in the New Mexico and Indian Territories. Knowing that Republicans would never agree to anything that countenanced slavery's protection, that word was studiously avoided. Disputes involving the rights of slaveholders in the Southern territories would "be subject to judicial cognizance in the Federal courts," those tribunals presided over by Republican appointees.

Tyler backed a plan requiring court appointments under the compromise to be ratified by a majority vote of the Senate, but with free-state senators approving nominees in the northern territories, slave-state senators in the southern. Though Tyler considered this "well calculated to heal discontents both North and South," the proposal failed.

Other points in the convention's narrowly approved plan dealt with maintaining slavery in the District of Columbia, compensating for runaways and prohibiting Congress from abolishing slavery in any state where it already existed. Many in the North refused to consider even these concessions. Maine, New Hampshire, Vermont, Massachusetts, Connecticut and Iowa voted "no" on nearly every item. North Carolina and Virginia would vote against the plan, knowing full well it offered too little to the departed states.[16]

Despite his disappointments Tyler continued to be in close consultation with President Buchanan. On the eve of the observance of Washington's birthday the president asked Tyler if he thought parading federal troops together with militia volunteers might create problems. Clearly, neither man wanted anything to upset prospects for peace, however dim those hopes were becoming.[17] During its deliberations a delegation from the Peace Convention had called on Buchanan. As those delegates neared the end of their work it seemed only fitting to pay the same courtesy to the president-elect. Several Southern members objected, but Tyler insisted on making the gesture.

Lincoln arrived in the capital the day after the celebration of Washington's birth and delegates came to see him at nine that evening at Willard's Hotel. Salmon P. Chase made the introductions, beginning with former President Tyler. Lincoln attempted to keep the conversation in a light vein, avoiding commitment, deflecting any discussion of the issues. Virginian James A. Seddon would have none of this. Cutting through the pleasantries the former Democratic congressman accused Lincoln of holding extreme views, implying that he supported John Brown's terrorism. This Lincoln cooly denied.

Then William E. Dodge, prominent New York City businessman, turned to the future president and spoke at length, demanding assurances of peace. "Now," he concluded, "it is for you, sir, to say whether the whole nation shall be plunged into bankruptcy, whether the grass shall grow in the streets of our commercial cities."

"Then I say it shall not," replied Lincoln. "If it depends upon me," he added with a pinch of sarcasm, "the grass shall not grow anywhere except in the fields and the meadows."

"Then you will yield to the just demands of the South," exclaimed Dodge. "You will not go to war on account of slavery!"

Lincoln bristled at the challenge. It had been a long day and his patience was wearing thin. He reminded everyone in the room that on taking office he would swear to " preserve, protect and defend" the Constitution. "The Constitution will not be preserved and defended until it is enforced and obeyed in every part of every one of the United States. It must be so respected, obeyed, enforced and defended, let the grass grow where it may."

Republicans in the room made no attempt to hide their delight at Lincoln's strong words. Several Southern delegates had heard enough and walked out, perhaps shaking their heads as they considered how Northern failure to respect and obey the Constitution had in fact brought them to this juncture. It seemed clear that Lincoln was willing to use force against Americans who declined to remain in his Union.

Tyler lingered as the president-elect was questioned further. What if the people of a territory chose slavery, asked a New Jersey delegate. Would that territory ever be allowed to become a slave state?

"It will be time to consider that question when it arises," he replied. Now we have other questions which we must decide. In a choice of evils, war may not always be the worst."[18]

Tyler was stunned. To Lincoln bloodshed seemed preferable to simply conceding Southern rights. Here was a man who could not be reasoned with. He denied self-determination to fellow Americans and would plunge the continent into war before he would compromise. The Virginian's last shred of hope for saving the old Union was gone.

A salute of one-hundred guns honored delegates as they adjourned in Washington, and stock markets rallied at the prospect of settlement. Though Tyler was bitterly disappointed in the proposals and had no confidence they could restore the Union, he felt an obligation to give them his official blessing. On February 27 he presented the recommendations to Congress. A committee chaired by Crittenden gave its approval, but the whole Senate rejected the amendment by a large margin. The House of Representatives was busy with other matters and failed to muster the two-thirds vote needed to interrupt its regular order of business.[19] The Peace Convention's work had done nothing but give a false hope to conservatives and slow secession's progress in the Upper South.

The Union of his fathers might be lost but there was still a chance, thought Tyler, of avoiding war by manipulating the balance of power. It was an idea he had toyed with for weeks and now embraced wholeheartedly. Back in January he suggested that should compromise fail the South might hold a convention and amend the Constitution to guarantee "justice" and future "security." Then, under the Stars and Stripes, with essentially the old Constitution, the South could invite whichever states would to join this new and reformed United States of America. It went without saying that the stratagem would effectively expel troublesome New England from the Union. During February Tyler's thinking continued to evolve. If the Peace Convention failed then Virginia should secede with the rest of the Upper South, possibly bringing two or more Northern states along. Such a combination would be far too powerful to be coerced by what remained of Lincoln's United States.[20]

Lincoln in his carefully worded March 4 inaugural address denied the legality of secession, as Buchanan had done. But, unlike Buchanan, Lincoln seemed to suggest that the federal government might force a state to return to the Union, vowing as he did to everywhere "enforce the laws" and "collect the revenues." In the new Confederacy his threats were taken as a virtual declaration of war. Upper South unionists preferred to dwell on what was not said. "*It is not a war message*," decided the *North Carolina Standard* of Raleigh. "It is not, strictly speaking, a Black Republican message; for while he recognizes slavery in the States as perpetual...he deliberately refrains from pressing...the exclusion of the South from all the Territories of the Union."[21]

Tyler was sure he understood Lincoln's true intentions. Taking his seat in the Virginia convention he urged, successfully, that the compromise be rejected. The Virginia convention also passed resolutions urging

United States recognition of the Confederate States and removal of Union military personnel from installations within the Confederacy. Tyler spoke to the delegates on March 13 and 14, his remarks made over a two-day period due to the state of his health. He was an "old man" brought out of retirement, "startled by...the voice of Virginia appealing to a son..." All hope of constitutional compromise was gone, he said. For the sake of liberty and her future prosperity the Old Dominion must now make common cause with the whole South. Virginia must immediately secede.

Elected to the convention by a conservative constituency, Tyler—a man in search of accommodation—had come back from the sobering confrontation in Washington a determined disunionist. The secessionist minority in the Virginia convention had gained a prominent recruit. Still, he was only one man, despite his stature and eloquence. Fellow Virginians listened respectfully but took no action.[22]

———

Down in Montgomery the Provisional Congress of the Confederate States had chosen a flag for the new Republic. A plethora of drawings had been submitted. One by Congressman William Porcher Miles featured a star-spangled, blue Saint Andrew's cross on a field of red. Someone joked that it resembled a "pair of suspenders" and it was rejected. The design finally chosen reminded many of the "old flag." In the blue canton was a circle of seven white stars, one for each state. Across the field stretched three broad horizontal bars—red, white and red.

A flag-raising ceremony was scheduled for the afternoon of March 4, the very day Congress had adopted the design, so a seamstress quickly set to work. Within two hours the first "Stars and Bars" was ready. Ceremonies began at three o'clock with the band playing a selection of sentimental and patriotic favorites. Seven young ladies, one representing each state of the new Confederacy, prepared to assist in unfurling the flag from atop the dome of the capitol. Newly sworn-in President Jefferson Davis chose for the honor of personally raising the flag a beautiful nineteen year old who happened to be in Montgomery staying with relatives—Letitia Christian Tyler, granddaughter of the former United States president.

The great clock above the portico struck four. With the last chime came the thunder of a cannon salute. Miss Tyler pulled the halyard, the flag went up and caught the breeze as thousands cheered.

The bandmaster raised his baton and the musicians began to play again. The crowd seemed to love it. The tune was a catchy minstrel number, only recently orchestrated, called "I Wish I Was in Dixie's Land."[23]

Swept Away by the Deluge
John Adams Gilmer

The rich wood paneling, elaborate decor and gas lighting in the new House chamber did little to dispel the icy tension in the air. It was late January 1861 in Washington City. Outside, lifeless trees lined muddy streets. The capitol grounds was littered with building materials and tools as work continued on the structure's exterior and massive dome. Members of the House of Representatives had been in their commodious south wing a little over three years. But now there seemed to be more empty desks each day. All around Washington this "secession winter" Southerners were resigning their seats, packing, preparing to depart for home. Congressmen from Southern states still in the Union anxiously groped for a solution, lashing out alternately at "secessionist hotheads" and "Black Republicans."

"We are resolved to have all the rights guaranteed to us by our forefathers," declared John B. Clark, Missouri congressman. The fifty-eight year old from Fayette in Howard County had gone over his allotted time and Republican members could only be angered by his threatening manner. This Border State representative demanded that they — the victorious party — accept compromise if they expected to halt the dissolution of the country. Five states had already declared independence. Even as he spoke, on this January twenty-sixth, convention delegates in Baton Rouge were voting for Louisiana's secession. "If we cannot secure our rights in the present confederation," Clark concluded, "we will be compelled to confederate where they can be secured."[2]

Then John Adams Gilmer came to his feet. Gilmer was of medium height, muscular, with a round face, dark hair and dark eyes. Those

John Adams Gilmer

"deep-set and laughing dark eyes" said one who knew him, displayed "intelligence, energy, and kindness." Before representing his North Carolina district in the United States Congress he had been a prosperous attorney in the Greensboro area, but a man who never forgot his humble country background. Friends described a "bluff, frank and cordial" man full of "hope, confidence and cheerfulness." Today there was only sadness in his eyes. Earlier in the month he had confessed to a friend that the state of the country was such that "I often shed tears in silence."[3]

He began by pointing the finger of blame at fellow Southerners for what was happening. For decades South Carolina had been "conspiring for disunion" until now the storm of secession raged all around them, growing in strength, threatening the country he loved. Southerners in the Border States were being told that only in political separation was there "safety." An argument "equally fallacious, equally dangerous" held that secession of the entire South would soon be followed by the reconstruction of a new and better Union. Both were lies used by disunionists to cover up their true intentions. These "ultra men" had no fear of Republican refusal to compromise. In fact, Gilmer charged, secessionists demanded protection of slavery in the territories only because they knew it would be refused. Once refused, they could then further inflame Southern opinion.

Gilmer turned to Republicans in the chamber. "I would say to my northern friends...that you have it in your power...to crush this thing out in one hour." Simply allow both sections equal rights to the territories and there would be "a speedy end to the ambitious schemes of disunion politicians." The endless debate was no more than "an excuse for agitation" that accomplished nothing. "I incline to the opinion that in the future, as heretofore, soil, climate, and productions would settle this question of slavery in the Territories, if peace and quiet were restored. After all that has been said and done, Congress has never made a free State out of any Territory that nature intended for a slave State, and has never made a slave State out of territory where free labor could be profitably employed."

Gilmer pleaded with his Republican colleagues to consider *any* compromise, *any* concession that might deprive secessionists of their arguments. Southern fears were real and would continue to be exploited if Republicans kept silent or ignored the problem.

"You say you have elected your President constitutionally," said the North Carolinian. "I admit it. You express wonder and surprise that the South should be alarmed at this. Now, let me reason with you...Suppose the position of the two sections of the Union was reversed; suppose the slave States were eighteen, and the free States fifteen; suppose the slave States had a majority in this House, a majority in the Senate, and a majority in the electoral college; suppose the slave States were to hold a convention, and appoint the place of meeting as far South as they could, say at Mobile; that there should be no delegates in that convention from the free States;

that they should nominate two candidates, one from Florida and the other from Texas, and should wind up their proceedings by the adoption of a resolution intimating that it is in the power of Congress, as well as the duty of Congress, to provide that no more free States shall be admitted into the Union, and should elect their candidates nominated by the slave States alone; suppose all these things were to happen, and then speeches, assurances, and telegrams, should be freely circulated throughout your country, that the South intend to make all the States slaveholding States: I submit to you, my northern friends, would you not be very much warmed up against that southern movement, and begin to feel that you were but small folks in this Government? Would you not feel like looking out for yourselves, at least to the extent of asking for some guarantees?"

Settlement of every sectional dispute was within reach if only the time-honored spirit of compromise could be revived. "Is it possible that the sons of American fathers cannot agree on this trifling matter?" What would the Founding Fathers do under these circumstances? Would they let matters go on until blood was shed? "Why, they would settle this question immediately. They would not go to dinner before they had settled it."

Should compromise fail and conflict come, Gilmer knew it would be his duty to stand by North Carolina. But in disunion he saw only war in all of its horror. "I want gentlemen North and South to mark my words: when...this country shall be laid waste; when all our channels and communications of trade shall be broken up; when the shipping in our ports shall be destroyed; when our institutions of learning and religion shall wither away or be torn down; when your cities shall be given up for plunder and for slaughter; when your sons and my sons, your neighbors and my neighbors, shall be carried from this bloody field of strife; and our mothers, our sisters, our wives, and our daughters, shall assemble around us, and, with weeping eyes and aching hearts, say: 'Could not you have done something, could not you have said something, that would have averted this dreadful calamity?' I want to feel in my conscience and in my soul that I have done my duty."

As Gilmer finished, dozens of Southern unionists and sympathetic Republicans came charging down the aisles to clasp his hand and slap him on the back. Never, said one reporter, had he witnessed "such an effect as was produced" by the "honest appeal of a great heart." One Republican congressman resolved then and there that "some compromise must be made to keep John A. Gilmer from being carried down by the secession tide."[4]

———

One congressional colleague from Lincoln's party pronounced Gilmer "a man of great personal popularity and ability." As candidate in a losing bid for Speaker of the House, Gilmer had attempted to keep the issue of slavery out of the contest. In 1860 he became chairman of the Committee on Elections, with Republican support. Two years earlier he had voted against the pro-slavery Lecompton Constitution proposed for Kansas. It took courage to vote against the interests of his own section, but he felt that the document did not truly express the will of the people of the territory. John Adams Gilmer was indeed one Southerner most Republicans could respect.

From his first election to the state legislature Gilmer had built a solid unionist reputation, first as a Whig and then in the American Party. He made an unsuccessful run for the governorship in 1856, creating a good impression in the attempt. Gilmer had studied law after briefly teaching school in South Carolina. The new lawyer grew wealthy through fortunate investments in railroads and coal mines, and by his wife Julianna's inheritance. Though he would come to own over fifty slaves himself, the county he came from was dominated by small farmers with little interest in the concerns of planters. His Scotch-Irish family had been in the Greensboro area for generations and both of Gilmer's grandfathers fought in the battle of Guilford Courthouse during the revolutionary war. Born during the Jefferson administration, the eldest of twelve children, his father's politics can perhaps be discerned in his naming his first born for the defeated Federalist president.[5]

Though "stiff-backed" Republicans balked at any talk of compromise, a few in the party were listening to the warnings of Gilmer and others. Surprisingly, prominent among these emerging moderates was William Henry Seward. Seward's image as a radical who might alienate Northern conservatives had cost him the 1860 nomination, Republicans turning to the less well-known Lincoln. Still, Seward's political clout made it expedient for Lincoln to offer him the State Department, first place in the cabinet.

If secession could be confined to the Deep South, concluded Seward, the movement might lose its momentum and eventually be rolled back. Conciliation was new to the man of "irrepressible conflict" fame. But Seward came to understand that unionists in the Upper South must be strengthened if further disintegration and war were to be avoided. What better way to bind the sections together than to name a Southerner to the cabinet? Seward sent his friend Thurlow Weed to the president-elect to sound him out on the idea. Lincoln was cool and initially noncommittal. It might be risky to pick a non-Republican. And it seemed unlikely that a Southerner of any stature could be found who might accept. Besides, what if the man's state should secede? Newspaperman Weed did not give up, proposing the names of two former congressmen from Virginia and Tennessee and two presently-serving representatives from Maryland and North Carolina. The North Carolinian he recommended was Gilmer.

Lincoln knew something of the man, having just a week before received a letter from him. Gilmer had the advantage of being currently in office, and North Carolina was the southern-most of the states considered, sharing no border with a free state. Lincoln would give it a try, though the offer must be kept a secret. He told Weed that he would write to Gilmer, state his views, and if the congressman was agreeable, invite him to join the cabinet.[6]

From Washington on December 10 — before any secession convention had convened — Gilmer had written to Lincoln in Springfield, Illinois. He began by apologizing, as a political opponent, for taking the liberty of "troubling you with any inquiries." Gilmer had, after all, supported Bell for president. What the North Carolinian hoped for were assurances that would calm Southern apprehensions and head off disunion. Gilmer questioned Lincoln on a number of delicate issues. Would the new president categorically veto the admission of future slave states? Would he enforce the Fugitive Slave Law? Did Lincoln believe Congress had the authority to interfere with slavery in the states? Gilmer felt that "a clear and definite exposition" of Lincoln's views "may go far to quiet, if not satisfy all reasonable minds." And by yielding on a few points "more abstract than useful or practical" the new majority party might achieve "the preservation of the best Government that has ever fallen to the lot of any people."[7]

Lincoln answered Gilmer's letter on December 15, before the cabinet offer came up. He began by saying that he hesitated even to touch on the issues raised, but feared Gilmer "might misconstrue my silence." No new statements were needed, said Lincoln bluntly, since all of his views were on record. "It is all in print and easy of access." The president-elect claimed that he and Gilmer's major difference was over slavery in the territories. "You think slavery is right and ought to be extended," said Lincoln somewhat presumptuously, "we think it is wrong and ought to be restricted."[8]

Lincoln wrote again to Gilmer later in the month, asking the congressman to visit him in Springfield, but the invitation arrived in Washington after Gilmer had returned home to North Carolina for Christmas. A clerk finally relayed the information to Gilmer on December 29. The North Carolinian had no idea that Lincoln wanted him in the cabinet and he could not understand why the president-elect asked for a face-to-face meeting. Gilmer immediately replied with a letter begging Lincoln to understand how serious the secession crisis had become. South Carolina was out and would quickly be followed by Georgia, Florida, Alabama and Mississippi. But, said Gilmer, if Lincoln quickly adopted a conciliatory attitude on slavery in the territories and recommended a constitutional amendment to protect slavery in the states the contagion of disunion might be contained.

When Gilmer returned to Washington a few days later he was informed first by Seward and later by Weed that he was being considered for a post in the cabinet. It was apparently understood that he would either take the Treasury Department or become secretary of the navy. Gilmer did not quite know what to do. Were there not, he asked Seward, Southerners more suitable? No, Lincoln preferred him. The North Carolinian confidentially sought the advice of other unionists in his own state and elsewhere. The consensus was that he weigh the offer carefully, and certainly not reject it out of hand. Former North Carolina Congressman Edwin G. Reade "strongly urged Mr. Gilmer to accept." Maryland Representative Henry Winter Davis, one Republican who was defeated in 1860, recommended the appointment as crucial to the cause of Southern unionism. It was "a matter of life or death," insisted Davis, that Gilmer take the job.[9]

Two weeks later Lincoln stated to a third party that he thought well of Gilmer and hoped he would accept the cabinet post. Twice during February, after Gilmer's emotional House speech, Lincoln told visitors that Gilmer was still his man. But the congressman remained undecided. Political advancement meant little now to Gilmer. His letters were filled with pleas for moderation and peace. He felt he could not join hands with the Republican administration without assurances Lincoln would do everything he could to hold on to the Upper South. If Lincoln could only grasp the fact that "slavery in the territories" was a non-issue, nothing but a rallying cry for extremists on both sides. Gilmer believed that it was up to the Republicans, the party soon to be in power, to take the initiative by making concessions. Weed frankly told the president-elect that Republican intransigence only helped secessionists while undermining friends of the Union in the Upper South. Seward seemed conciliatory and that raised Gilmer's hopes, but still Lincoln stubbornly refused to make the effort Gilmer thought was needed. "There must be no fighting," Gilmer pleaded to Seward, "or the conservative Union men in the border slave states...who are at this time largely in the majority, will be swept away in a torrent of madness."[10]

"Northern extreme men are working night and day to defeat all compromises," Gilmer wrote to a friend. "Southern extreme men do the same thing, and daily write letters, and send telegraph dispatches out South to excite & inflame our people to the utmost tension. The fury & madness of the South becomes hourly more and more aggravated." Gilmer would do all he could to counter secessionist sentiment in North Carolina. Conspiring with the sympathetic Census Bureau chief to procure names and addresses, Gilmer prepared a mass-mailing of unionist literature. He used his franking privilege for postage, but otherwise paid for everything out of his own pocket. It took twenty clerks working late into many nights, but eventually 100,000 North Carolinians were reading his views on the crisis. Angry secessionists shouted in protest that "Gilmer and company" were in league with "the Census Bureau and the Black Republicans" to promote "submission and coercion."[11]

Just before the presidential inauguration Gilmer was shown a draft of Lincoln's address. Rather than the conciliatory message he prayed for, Gilmer read an ironclad reaffirmation of Republican opposition to slavery in the territories. Most ominous was Lincoln's vow to retake federal property that had been seized in the seceded states. Coercion seemed his intent. Disquieting too was the announcement that Salmon P. Chase would be Lincoln's secretary of the treasury. The Ohioan had a long record of antislavery activism and his appointment looked like one more indication that moderation was not to be the administration's policy. Gilmer made up his mind. He could not accept a cabinet position.[12]

II.

Just two days before Lincoln was to take the oath of office Seward informed the president-elect that he would not be serving as secretary of state. Lincoln's appointment of Chase and the equally radical Montgomery Blair to his cabinet did nothing, held Seward, to help the unionist cause in the Upper South. And the draft that he read of the inaugural address could but leave him shaking his head. "All the power at my disposal," Lincoln had written, "will be used to reclaim the public property and places which have fallen..." The Deep South could not be isolated and loyalty in the Upper South strengthened by threats, argued Seward. Lincoln gave in. He would moderate his inaugural language (if not his views) if that would induce Seward to stay on. There must be no rupture within Republican ranks on the eve of taking the reins of power. In the revised version Lincoln vowed only "to hold, occupy and possess" government property and "to collect the duties and imposts" while promising "no invasion, no using of force against or among the people anywhere." When Gilmer finally heard these moderated words he was relieved. "What more," he asked, "does any reasonable Southern man expect or desire?"[13]

Other Upper South conservatives seconded Gilmer and continued to urge that "reasonable" Southerners stand by the Union. Agreeing with Lincoln that no right of secession existed, the Nashville *Republican Banner* referred pointedly to the new Confederacy as the "Revolutionary Cotton States." Secessionists could hardly complain about "coercion," said the *Banner*, since by seizing property belonging to the United States they were themselves "coercing" the federal government. The *Daily Nashville Patriot* was already on record as an enemy of any who promoted disunion. Secession, wrote the editor, "is a nullity in law," resistance to the Union "a crime." The conservative editor of the Raleigh *North Carolina Standard* had long since taken his stand for the Union at any price but "honor and Constitutional rights." Answering secessionist critics he conceded that resistance to tyranny might one day be the only option. "*But not now!* — the nonslaveholder says *not now!* — the slaveholder, whose property civil war would involve in imminent peril, says *not now!* — millions of our friends in the free States say *not now!*"[14]

On the day Lincoln took up residence in the White House the only remaining outposts of federal authority in the seven-state Confederacy were isolated Forts Pickens, Taylor and Jefferson in Florida; and Fort Sumter in Charleston Harbor. If there was to be a collision between opposing forces it was likely to begin in secession's birthplace, South Carolina.

With the state's withdrawal from the Union Major Robert Anderson, commanding federal installations near Charleston, was put in a precarious position. His small garrison was headquartered at Fort Moultrie on Sullivan's Island, protecting the entrance to the harbor. Moultrie was in poor shape. Multistory vacation homes dominated its walls and sand piled up against the fort allowed even cows to stray inside. Anderson also had responsibility for obsolete Castle Pinckney, the arsenal in the city and a construction project called Fort Sumter.

Fort Sumter was named in honor of the legendary revolutionary war patriot Thomas Sumter. Called "the Gamecock," General Sumter lived long enough to endorse nullification in the 1830s. Work on the fort had been going on for over thirty years, slowed by congressional reluctance to spend money on national defense during peacetime. When finished, its 146 guns were to command the channel, guarding Charleston from invasion by any foreign enemy. In December 1860 it was still under construction, ungarrisoned and only partially armed, though work crews continued their labors.[15]

A career soldier with an ingrained loyalty to the Stars and Stripes of the Union, Anderson was born in Kentucky, married a Georgian, had owned slaves and sympathized with the South's grievances. Chosen to be a diplomat in the sensitive Charleston post, he was given an impossible task.

Before Anderson arrived at his new command Lieutenant General Winfield Scott mentioned to him that Sumter seemed more secure than Moultrie. Yet the major was ordered by the secretary of war not "to take up any position which could be construed into the assumption of a hostile attitude." But if attacked, or if "you have tangible evidence" that an attack might come, he was free to put all of his command into one fort. South Carolina's secession, and state guardboats patrolling the harbor, seemed all the "tangible evidence" he needed. On the night of December 26 he spiked Moultrie's cannons, burned the gun carriages, cut down the flagpole and moved his eighty-four men in secrecy to the island bastion of Fort Sumter. Surrounded by water, protected by tall brick walls, he and his men for the moment felt triumphantly secure. In the morning the crew of the guardboat *Nina* realized the Federals had slipped away and they raced to the city with the news. Governor Pickens complained that there had been an informal agreement with Washington not to disturb the status quo. President Buchanan was embarrassed by the major's move, but declined to send him back. The governor retaliated by having his militiamen occupy Moultrie, Castle Pinckney and take possession of the arsenal's 22,000 muskets.[16]

Leaders of the Palmetto State were anxious to negotiate for Sumter and the other installations, if the United States would only recognize South

Carolina's new status. The same day that Anderson made his move, commissioners Robert W. Barnwell, James L. Orr and James Hopkins Adams set up a sort of "South Carolina embassy" at 352 K Street in Washington. South Carolina had ceded the land for the forts back in 1805 on condition the installations be used for the state's defense. The commissioners contended that an independent Palmetto State no longer required the U.S. Army to defend the harbor. South Carolina wanted to reclaim the land, but was willing to pay for the forts themselves.[17]

Buchanan was in no mood to listen to any of South Carolina's arguments. He first convinced himself that Anderson ought to be reinforced by a warship and more troops. Then he changed his mind, but decided to send in secretly a load of supplies. A merchant ship called *The Star of the West* was chartered in New York. When word of the mission leaked out the president tried to stop the *Star* from sailing, but it was too late. On Morris Island, overlooking the approaches to the harbor but beyond the range of Sumter's guns, Governor Pickens had ordered the erection of a battery of four 24-pound field howitzers. Manned by forty cadets from the South Carolina Military Academy, protected by a infantry company of state militia, the battery was ready when the *Star* arrived at dawn on January 9. Cadet George Haynesworth pulled his lanyard, one gun thundered and jumped in response, sending a shot splashing across the ship's bow. When she ignored the warning more shots followed, two iron projectiles splintering the wooden hull before her captain retreated to safety. Anderson was furious. The United States flag had been fired upon and he was helpless to stop it. He could have retaliated by opening up on Moultrie, sealing the harbor or even by shelling the city. Instead, he complained to Pickens. The governor's reply curtly informed the major that he, by his very presence in South Carolina, was the aggressor. The *Star* episode resulted in a truce that bought time for Pickens to strengthen his batteries.[18] For his part, Buchanan was only too glad to let matters drag on. In less than eight weeks he could turn over the explosive situation to his successor.

From Sumter's walls Captain Abner Doubleday of the U.S. Army, abolitionist firebrand from New York, frowned with contempt on what Carolinians saw as their sacred symbols of liberty. Not until the end of January would the South Carolina General Assembly choose a white palmetto and crescent on a blue field as the design for the state's flag. It would be a tribute to a similar banner flown from Colonel William Moultrie's palmetto-log fort when patriots defeated the British fleet in 1776. But for now individualism and imagination ruled. A palmetto flag with a red field flew from the cadet battery. Moultrie's repaired flagpole displayed a banner with a green palmetto tree and red star on a white field. Doubleday complained of seeing "nothing but uncouth State flags, representing palmettos, pelicans, and other strange devices...Our glasses in vain swept the horizon; the one flag we longed to see was not there..." When the new official state flag went up at Moultrie, Yankee Captain John Foster said that the white-and-blue banner brought to mind the "Jolly Roger." "It is not a handsome or pleasant flag to look at," reported the New Englander.[19]

The Stars and Bars of the Confederate States soon joined the palmetto flag on the forts and batteries surrounding Sumter. On March first Brigadier General Pierre Gustave Toutant Beauregard arrived in Charleston to assume command of South Carolina forces. Before secession the Louisiana native had been serving as a major in the United States Army. Now the West Point graduate and Mexican War veteran got down to the job of strengthening the batteries, preparing to take the fort and repel any federal invasion that might be attempted.[20]

———

The second session of the Thirty-sixth Congress adjourned on March 3, 1861. John Gilmer, concerned about illness in his family, started for home. He was still very much worried about the state of the country. His patience with secessionists was gone. "S.C. will not remain in harmony long in any Confederacy," he angrily concluded. "I pray that she may never come back." Over the next few days Gilmer bombarded Seward with letters. Repeatedly he warned the secretary that holding Fort Sumter and the other outposts of federal authority in the new Confederacy only hurt the Union's cause in the Upper South. Secessionists there warned incessantly of federal coercion. Should a fight break out over Sumter Gilmer knew that Southern states still in the Union would be forced to side with their sister states of the Deep South. Abandoning the forts should not be thought of as recognition of secession's legitimacy, Gilmer insisted. Leave the seceded states in peace. "The present excitement should be allowed to pass away as soon as possible, without fighting." Within two years they would discover that independence was not a panacea after all and be ready to return to the Union. Simply put, the best way to strengthen Upper South unionism was to leave the Deep South alone.[21]

Upon taking office Lincoln discovered that Fort Sumter was fast running out of supplies. Major Anderson estimated that it would take a federal army of no fewer than 20,000 to relieve the fort. Evacuation was the advice most of the cabinet gave to Lincoln and withdrawal orders were even prepared. Lincoln was in a quandary. He would make no immediate decision, keeping all options open.[22]

In early March three Confederate commissioners arrived in Washington charged with authority to negotiate differences between the two countries. Seward, at Lincoln's insistence, would not meet with them. But the secretary truly believed the president would soon come around to his way of thinking. Confidently, he told Supreme Court Justice John Campbell that Sumter was to be evacuated in three days. Campbell relayed this to the commissioners and they promptly informed President Davis.

The news of Anderson's imminent departure was believed in the South. Troops stopped work on the Charleston batteries and fired salutes in celebration. The major too assumed it was true and thanked God that "the separation which has been inevitable for months, will be consummated without the shedding of one drop of blood." Since war was thus avoided he hoped that the departed states "may at some future time be won back by conciliation and justice." When the deadline passed Campbell went again to the secretary and was met with more smiling assurances. Anderson was visited on March 24 by Ward H. Lamon, a friend of Lincoln's, who also left the impression that evacuation was still imminent. Believing they would leave momentarily, the major even stopped rationing his men's food supply.[23]

Seward was far out on a limb with his promises. He had expected to dominate the administration and in his dealings with the Confederates wanted to give the impression of being in charge. Now he had to face the fact that not only was he not making key decisions, he did not even know what his president was going to do. Unless Sumter was abandoned very soon, Seward's pretensions would be exposed. On All Fool's Day the secretary, in all seriousness, penned "Some Thoughts for the President's Consideration." He began by lamenting that, "We are at the end of a month's administration, and yet without a policy either domestic or foreign." He urged the evacuation of Sumter, the reinforcement of more isolated Florida posts and preparation for a naval blockade of the seceded states. The United States should then make impossible demands of France and Spain that would promptly lead to war with those powers. A foreign conflict, presumably, would serve to reunite the country. Politely but firmly, Lincoln rejected his secretary's unsolicited advice.[24]

The weeks of indecision finally were over. The president made up his mind about Sumter. To abandon the fort might very well be taken as recognition of secession's permanence. Northern supporters would be demoralized. After all, even Buchanan had kept the flag flying at Charleston. A retreat would damage Union prestige around the world. Despite warnings by Southern unionists, he concluded that the country might never recover should he back down now.

In a military sense Sumter could not be held permanently — that would require more troops than Lincoln had at his command. But he would not give it up without a fight. Time was running out. Anderson would have to quit if not resupplied. An attempt at reinforcement or resupply, even the threat of aid, would prompt Confederates to act. And if the use of force was called for and could not be avoided — if war was inevitable — then why not let the South fire the first shot? Nothing would do more to unite the North. The news of impending reinforcement would suffice to set events in motion.[25]

Lincoln would not acknowledge the existence of the Confederate States by communicating with their government, so he directed a note to

Governor Pickens. One Robert Chew, State Department clerk, arrived by rail in South Carolina's Port City on the evening of April 8 and went directly to the governor's office at the Charleston Hotel on Meeting Street. "I am directed by the President of the United States," read the missive handed to Pickens, "to notify you to expect an attempt will be made to supply Fort Sumter with provisions only, and that if such attempt be not resisted, no effort to throw in men, arms or ammunition, will be made, without further notice, or in case of an attack upon the Fort." The letter carried no salutation, no close, no signature. To drive home his contempt, Lincoln would only speak to secessionists through a clerk who was under orders to receive no reply. Anderson got the news in the mail. The turnaround in policy "would produce most disastrous results throughout the country," concluded the major. "We shall strive to do our duty, though I frankly say that my heart is not in the war which I see is to be thus commenced."[26]

President Davis could not allow a foreign fleet of eight ships armed with twenty-six guns and transporting 1,400 men to make a mockery of Southern independence by resupplying or reinforcing Sumter. The ships would arrive about April 15, the day Anderson estimated his food would run out. Confederates had no alternative but to "fire the first shot." Beauregard was ordered by his government to demand Sumter's evacuation, "and if this is refused, proceed in such manner as you may determine to reduce it." The Confederate commander offered Anderson generous terms, proposing that he and his men salute their flag upon leaving and be transported to any post in the Union. "But the Confederate States," the general emphasized, "can no longer delay assuming actual possession of a fortification commanding the entrance of one of their harbors and necessary to its defence and security." Anderson refused. He had a duty to perform.[27]

Out on Morris Island, at the Cummings Point Battery, the old "fire-eater" Edmund Ruffin had been named an honorary soldier of the Palmetto Guards and told he could fire the first gun. He was more than ready. Before Lincoln's inauguration he left Virginia and traveled to South Carolina so as not to live even a day under "Black Republican" rule. At half past four on the morning of April 12, 1861 a mortar shell burst directly above Fort Sumter, signaling the other batteries to open fire. With a gleam in his eyes Ruffin jerked the lanyard of his Columbiad. There was a mighty roar and a few seconds later an eight-inch shell exploded on the parapet of Fort Sumter. A general bombardment was under way.[28]

For the next two and one-half hours Confederate guns and mortars pounded the fort without Anderson defending himself. At daylight Sumter's guns began returning fire, to the cheers of the Southern gunners. All day and into the night the unequal duel continued. The relief expedition dispatched by Lincoln arrived, but anchored out of range and gave no assistance to the hard-pressed Anderson. The next morning incendiary shot fired by the Confederates set Sumter's barracks ablaze. The flames quickly spread. About one-thirty that afternoon, choking from the smoke, fire threatening his powder magazine, Anderson gave up.[29]

Still allowed to fire a salute to his flag on taking it down the next day, during the ceremony a cannon exploded killing one U.S. soldier and wounding five others. They were the only serious casualties suffered by either side during the entire battle. As Anderson and his men were being ferried to the fleet offshore they steamed by Morris Island where the *Star of the West* had been turned back three months before. Today Confederates lined the beach in silence, hats off, in a show of respect for their gallant opponents.[30]

III.

On Saturday, April 13, news of Sumter's fall was received in Lexington, Virginia. Local secessionists celebrated by erecting a flagpole in front of the Rockbridge County Courthouse and running up a Confederate flag. Unionists were in the majority around Lexington and some of them decided to stage their own demonstration of loyalty in the aftermath of the fort's surrender. On the same courthouse grounds they put up a taller pole with an eagle on top and hoisted a United States flag. Tempers flared on both sides. Soon a scuffle broke out between some pro-secession cadets from nearby Virginia Military Institute and unionist locals. The unionists, described as "working men," roughed up the boys and the Stars and Stripes continued to wave over Lexington.[31]

Elsewhere in the Old Dominion State the surrender of Fort Sumter set off gun salutes and parades by Confederate sympathizers, but unionists held their ground. Virginia convention delegate Jubal Early observed that there was no change in the basic sentiment of the people. Noisy secessionists with "bands of music in the streets" did not represent "the masses of the people of Virginia." He and other conservatives hoped to adjourn the convention in mid-April. They expected a Border State conference to convene and work out an acceptable compromise. Time, thought unionists, was on their side.[32]

Over in Louisville, Kentucky the *Daily Journal* denounced the attack on Sumter. Confederate "revolutionists" were obviously trying to draw in other states by their action. But it would not work. Editor George Prentice predicted that President Lincoln would react "with prudence and self-control," thereby bolstering unionist sentiment in the South.[33]

Then came the proclamation.

On April 15 Abraham Lincoln signed a document claiming that the laws were being "obstructed" in the seven states of the Deep South "by combinations too powerful to be suppressed by the ordinary course of judicial proceedings." The "persons composing the combinations" were ordered to "disperse." To back up his words the president called on states remaining in the Union to send him a total of 75,000 troops.[34]

The response in the North was enthusiastic, volunteers everywhere stepping forward to "defend the flag." Citizens of the Confederate States rallied to their colors, most believing that Lincoln had deliberately brought on hostilities in order to pin the Union together with bayonets. President Davis, speaking to his cabinet members, expressed sardonic surprise "to find States referred to as 'persons composing combinations' and that the sovereign creators of the Federal Government, the [former] States of the Union, should be commanded by their agent to disperse."[35]

Kentucky Governor Beriah Magoffin responded to the proclamation, and the War Department's requisition for troops, on the same day it was received. "In answer I say emphatically Kentucky will furnish no troops for the wicked purpose of subduing her sister Southern States." Governor Claiborne Jackson of Missouri branded the call "illegal, unconstitutional, and revolutionary in its object, inhuman and diabolical." Arkansas would give Lincoln no help, said Governor Henry M. Rector. "The people of this Commonwealth are freemen, not slaves, and will defend to the last extremity their honor, lives, and property against Northern mendacity and usurpation." In Nashville Governor Isham G. Harris fired off a reply informing Washington that "Tennessee will not furnish a single man for purpose of coercion, but 50,000, if necessary, for the defense of our rights and those of our Southern brethren." The governor followed up with a long letter in which he called "the present coercive policy" of the Lincoln administration "a wanton and alarming usurpation of power." Virginia's Governor John Letcher at first doubted that the requisition was even genuine. "You have chosen," he concluded, "to inaugurate civil war," and Virginia would meet the challenge. "I can be no party to this wicked violation of the laws of the country and to this war upon the liberties of a free people," replied Governor John W. Ellis from Raleigh. "You can get no troops from North Carolina."[36]

"We shall not discuss the past," wrote the unionist editor of the *North Carolina Standard*. "We glory in our course as a Constitutional Union man. The Union men are, at least, 'guiltless of their country's blood.'" Lincoln's proclamation brings the country to the brink of revolution and war. "The Confederate States have grievously erred, – they fired the first gun at Charleston, – they provoked the war; admit all this, and still there is no justification for an attempt on the part of Mr. Lincoln to involve the whole country in war and bloodshed." It is now up to the states of the Upper South to "unite and command the peace, if possible; if we fail in that, *we must fight*."

The Daily Nashville Patriot still could not believe in a state's constitutional right to secede, but called for resistance to Lincoln based "upon the inherent right of revolution." *The Nashville Republican Banner* agreed, calling the theory of secession "an absurdity." But the time for revolution had come. "We repudiate and scorn and spit upon the men and the spirit by whom and by which the best government the world ever saw has been perverted into an engine of oppression to one half of its people, because they held an institution, recognized in the fundamental law, obnoxious to these Union savers." John Bell, 1860 presidential candidate of the Constitutional Union Party, agreed that Tennessee now had no choice but to join the Confederate States.

Lincoln's policy of coercion was "hare brained and ruinous," said the Louisville *Daily Journal*. The man was unfit to be president. "We are struck with mingled amazement and indignation. The policy announced in the Proclamation deserves the unqualified condemnation of every American citizen."[37]

In North Carolina one union leader was addressing the crowd at a political rally. Fort Sumter had just surrendered. The speaker raised his hand, emphasizing his plea for peace and continued loyalty to the Union. Just then came the shouted news of Lincoln's call for 75,000 volunteers. When his arm came down, in his own words, "it fell slowly and sadly by the side of a Secessionist."

"No man desired or worked harder than myself to preserve the Union," said conservative Jonathan Worth. "In North Carolina the Union sentiment was largely in the ascendant and gaining strength until Lincoln prostrated us." Now, he observed, North Carolina is "a perfect unit."[38]

Six days after the proclamation Gilmer wrote a letter to Seward. His tone was not angry or aggressive, only sad. Up until Lincoln's call for volunteers he and other unionists felt certain they could "overcome the disunionists in North Carolina." The "fight at Charleston had done us no harm." But Lincoln did "the very thing which the disunionists desired," the use of force extinguishing all of his hopes. "As matters now stand there is a United North against a United South, and both marching to the field of blood."[39]

On April 16 the crowd that had roughed up those V.M.I. cadets and raised the "Union pole" returned to the Rockbridge Courthouse. Quickly they set to work and soon their flagpole toppled to the ground. Five weeks later referendum returns showed that the county had voted 1,728 to 1 for secession.[40]

Down in the Palmetto State those original secessionists could not resist an "I-told-you-so" attitude. "That the brutal fanatics who sit in the high places at Washington are ready to plunge the whole country into contest and blood, we have never doubted," wrote the *Charleston Mercury* just after Lincoln's proclamation. "Events have shown that our estimation of this brutal and bloody faction was correct."[41]

The actions of Lincoln confirmed John Tyler in his impression of the man. "Mr. Lincoln, having weighed in the scales the value of a mere local Fort, against the value of the Union itself, resolved to send ships of war and

armed men to bring on that very collision which he well knew would arise..."
That no one was killed in the battle could only be understood, felt Tyler, as
a providential sign admonishing "against the inauguration of a bloody civil
war." But peace was not the Republican president's intention. Lincoln's
words, spoken at that confrontation in Washington two months earlier,
still burned in Tyler's ears. "In a choice of evils," he had said, "war may not
always be the worst." Tyler was certain that Lincoln had deliberately forced
the Confederates to act at Fort Sumter in order "to rally the masses of the
North around his own person and to prevent the faction which had brought
him into power from falling asunder. In this he has succeeded..."[42]

Virginia's convention passed an ordinance of secession on April 17,
subject to ratification by a vote of the people. The margin in favor of secession was 88 to 55, (103 to 46 when it came time to sign), most of the negative
tally coming from the mountainous western counties. The referendum passed
by a similar margin. The Confederacy had gained the most populous, indus-
trialized and prestigious state in the South. After the convention vote John
Tyler was escorted to the platform amid a standing, cheering ovation. He
declared that at no time in history had Virginians "engaged in a more just
and holy effort for the maintenance of liberty and independence."[43]

In Arkansas it took until May 6 to reconvene the convention. Delegates voted 70 to 1 for secession.[44]

Tennessee never called a convention, the legislature choosing to allow the people by direct vote to decide what was a foregone conclusion.
The Volunteer State's referendum avoided the issue of secession's constitutionality. The "Declaration of Independence" began by "waiving any
expression of opinion as to the abstract doctrine of secession, but asserting
the right, as a free and independent people, to alter, reform, or abolish our
form of government in such manner as we think proper..."[45]

In North Carolina a minority of conservatives among the former unionists, including delegate John Gilmer, insisted to the end that no right of
secession existed. Dissolving ties with the Union was now necessary, they
all agreed, but ought to be based on the people's fundamental right to overthrow tyranny. The distinction was overruled. North Carolina's vote came
five months to the day after South Carolina's. And, like their neighbors to
the south, North Carolina delegates voted unanimously for secession.[46]

Four days after Lincoln's proclamation a pro-Southern crowd in Baltimore attacked a Massachusetts regiment headed to Washington and a
number of civilians were shot. That night railroad bridges in the city were
burned. Despite widespread Confederate sentiment it seemed unlikely that
secessionists had the votes to force the issue in the Maryland legislature.
Federal authorities took no chances, arresting pro-secession lawmakers.
Newspapermen from Hagerstown to Baltimore suspected of favoring disunion were jailed. Secretary of State Seward, his short-lived "moderation"
now forgotten, allegedly bragged to the British ambassador about the wave

of arrests. The secretary had a little bell on his desk that he had only to ring to have anyone in the country arrested. Could the Queen do as much? he asked. Seward, concluded Her Majesty's Prime Minister, is a "vapouring, blustering, ignorant man."[47]

Most Missourians, even after April 15, wanted somehow to remain neutral and at peace. It was a futile hope. Governor Jackson stationed a seven-hundred-man force of militia near St. Louis that Nathaniel Lyon, commander of federal forces, thought threatened his arsenal. On May 10 Lyon and 6,000 troops surrounded the militiamen, took them captive and paraded them back to St. Louis. Confronted by outraged citizens, the soldiers opened fire. Jackson and his supporters then called for secession, but were forced to flee Jefferson City before Lyon's advancing army. The Missouri governor and a rump legislature would join the Confederacy, even as unionists clamped their hold on the state.[48]

Lincoln was reported to have said that "to lose Kentucky is nearly the same as to lose the whole game." The birthplace of both he and his counterpart Jefferson Davis, the state was rich in resources, population and strategically located. With Lincoln's proclamation the legislature "declared neutrality" but Kentucky became a battleground where unionists soon gained the upper hand. John C. Breckinridge remained at his post in the Senate, speaking out against Lincoln's war, until forced to flee Washington to avoid arrest. "The United States no longer exists," declared the former American vice president, now a hunted man. The Constitution "has been wholly abolished. It is as much forgotten as if it lay away back in the twilight of history."

Though they controlled little territory, in late 1861 secessionist Kentuckians established a revolutionary state government, voted to leave the Union and were promptly admitted to the Confederacy.[49] The Southern flag had gained its thirteenth star.

With the triumph of secession many who had taken no part in the political struggle that led to independence now stepped forward, motivations ranging from self-interest to an irresistible attachment to the place of their birth. "With all my devotion to the Union and the feeling of loyalty and duty of an American citizen," wrote Colonel Robert E. Lee three days after Virginia's secession, "I have not been able to make up my mind to raise my hand against my relatives, my children, my home." His was a common theme. Down in Charleston free blacks, many slaveholders themselves, declared that "our allegiance is due to South Carolina and in her defense, we will offer up our lives, and all that is dear to us." Even slaves routinely expressed loyalty to their homeland, thousands serving the Confederate Army faithfully. After a period of indecision and infighting the five civilized tribes of the Indian Territory—Cherokee, Chickasaw, Choctaw, Creek, and Seminole—joined ranks with the South.[50] The torrent had become a flood that swept all before it.

For a time some dreamed that American Presbyterians, united through the years of sectionalism, might somehow remain one denomination in two countries. It could not be. At the Philadelphia General Assembly in May 1861, with few Southerners able to attend, political pressure and patriotic enthusiasm carried the day. Resolutions proposed by Dr. Gardiner Spring of New York declared church support for the "integrity of these United States." Princeton's Dr. Charles Hodge and others protested, but in vain.[51]

The General Assembly having made loyalty to the United States a religious obligation, Southern members had little choice but to form their own denomination. On December 4 they met in Augusta, Georgia to establish the Presbyterian Church in the Confederate States of America.

Dr. Benjamin M. Palmer preached the opening sermon and served as moderator. Pastor of the host church, Rev. Joseph R. Wilson, no doubt hoped that the historic gathering would be remembered by his five-year-old son Woodrow. Certainly the most memorable event came near the end of the assembly when James Henley Thornwell moved to the platform. Weak and unwell, he was forced to lean against the pulpit for support. A hush fell over the congregation as he began to read an "Address of the Presbyterian Church in the Confederate States of America to All the Churches of Jesus Christ throughout the Earth." The statement was quintessential Thornwell, encompassing justification for the formation of the new denomination and an eloquent exposition of Southern Presbyterian perspectives. Once more, this time for an international audience, he made it clear that "in our ecclesiastical capacity, we are neither the friends nor the foes of Slavery." Thornwell extended the right hand of fellowship to Christians worldwide. "It is for you," he said, "to accept it or reject it."

No doubts or fears clouded his mind about the decisions he had made, the course he had run, the cause he now upheld. His words near the conclusion of the address, if taken in a secular sense, expressed sentiments that secessionists of all persuasions might recognize as their own.

"We have done our duty," spoke the preacher. "We can do no more. Truth is more precious than union..."[52]

Thomas Cooper would have shaken his head in amazement to see Columbia now. A quarter century after his death the South Carolina capital had more than doubled in population. Fine new homes and businesses lined streets that in Cooper's time cut through stands of pine trees. For a decade Columbians had watched in pride as the monumental new state capitol slowly took form at the intersection of Gervais and Richardson Streets. Town Hall, where Cooper spoke against the tariff and questioned the value of the Union, was still the city's center and most prominent landmark. From the tower the night watchman continued to keep a sharp eye out for fire.

In this late winter of 1865 all Columbians were preoccupied with the war. During four years of carnage every family in the city had been touched by death. Battlefield reverses and home-front shortages left most with a hard-eyed determination to keep on despite grinding poverty and hopeless odds. Reminders of the war were everywhere. Bales of unsold, blockaded cotton piled up on the streets. Convalescing soldiers, some missing arms or legs, were a common sight. Blue-clad prisoners huddled behind the red brick walls of the Insane Asylum. The war even forced Columbia to become a manufacturing center. Near the Congaree River, at a prudent distance from downtown, a mill made gunpowder. The Palmetto Iron Works produced cannon barrels, shot and shell. Other smaller factories scattered around town turned out rifles, buttons, bayonets and swords. The well-guarded firm of Keating & Ball printed currency and bonds for the Confederate Treasury Department.[1]

Yet Columbia and the rest of the South could not manufacture what they needed most: men to fill the depleted ranks. The enemy's numerical advantage each day became more overwhelming. After initial waves of volunteers went into uniform, conscription acts mobilized the Confederate

— 114 —

Nation for total war. Three-quarters of a million would serve the Southern cause, but still there was no way to counter the North's manpower resources. Perhaps as many as 260,000 Southerners — no one knew exactly how many — never came home.

The ladies of the capital city established two hospitals for the wounded, both strategically located near the railroad terminals. To raise funds they organized a "Great Bazaar," held in the state capitol during mid-January 1865. For six months they planned and worked to get ready. Railroad companies agreed to transport bazaar merchandise to Columbia at no charge. There were raffles, auctions and sales of food and handmade items. Each of the thirteen Confederate states had booths, though some of the overrun states were represented by local ladies. It was an opportunity once again to wave the tattered flag of Confederate patriotism and smile in the face of adversity.

Far from the front lines, Columbia had long been a place of refuge for civilians fleeing federal incursions along the coast and the shelling of Charleston. But the war drew ever closer. During the summer of 1864 Union General William Tecumseh Sherman had campaigned through northern Georgia, finally capturing and destroying Atlanta. After burning a path sixty miles wide through the southern part of that state, by early 1865 his 62,000 veterans were poised to invade South Carolina. Confederate defenders were badly outnumbered and "more or less demoralized" according to their commander. Sherman reported his army "crazy to be turned loose in Carolina," his men "burning with an insatiable desire to wreak vengeance" on the birthplace of secession.[2]

On February first Federals crossed the Savannah River and began their march on Columbia. Outnumbered nearly ten-to-one, Confederates made a stubborn stand at a place called Rivers Bridge, but were outflanked and forced to retreat. Every farm, village and town in Sherman's path was pillaged and torched. "The army burned everything it came near in the State of South Carolina," boasted an Illinois major, "not under orders, but in spite of orders."[3] The approach of Sherman's army was heralded not by banners, but by rising columns of smoke on the horizon.

———

The sight was spared James Henley Thornwell. He had returned home from the Augusta assembly to write a patriotic appeal distributed widely to Southern soldiers and civilians. Called "Our Danger and Our Duty," in it he predicted desolation of the country and the death of liberty should the Confederacy be defeated. His health broken, concerned about his son's battle wounds, Thornwell took refuge in the cooler climate of Lincoln County, North Carolina. He died there in August 1862. He was forty-nine years old.[4]

Neither would John Tyler witness his country's defeat. When Richmond became the Southern capital that first Confederate spring, the Virginia convention unanimously elected Tyler to the Provisional Congress. In November there would be elections for the House of Representatives under the permanent Constitution and the former United States president was persuaded to make the race. He issued an address to the voters of the Third District, reviewing the long march of liberty from Runnymeade to the American Revolution down to the perils of the present. Freedom, in his view, had disappeared in the United States under the Lincoln regime. "Those very people who basely submit to a despotism so unrelenting and cruel invade our soil without a shadow of right, and declare it to be their purpose to force us back into a union which they have destroyed, under a Constitution which they have rendered a mockery and made a nullity." Running against two opponents, Tyler received twice their combined vote.

On the night of January 9, 1862 Julia Tyler was awakened at her Sherwood Forest home, shaken by a vivid dream that her husband was deathly sick. Hurrying to join him at Richmond's Exchange Hotel, where he awaited the opening of Congress, the former First Lady was relieved to find him in apparent good health. Two days later the seventy-one-year-old Tyler became ill. He died on January 18 with Julia at his side. His body lay in state in the Confederate capitol as thousands filed past to pay their respects, his casket draped with the Stars and Bars. President Davis led mourners to Tyler's final resting place in Hollywood Cemetery, near to the grave of James Monroe. The passing of the former president of the United States was ignored in that country.[5]

After serving in the North Carolina convention John Adams Gilmer returned to private life. His only son and his younger brother donned gray uniforms. Gilmer, the man Lincoln had wanted for his cabinet, would be elected to the Second Congress of the Confederate States. Congressman Gilmer favored sending representatives to the Hampton Roads Conference in February 1865, a North-South parley that only proved that Lincoln would accept nothing short of Confederate surrender. For his part, Gilmer refused to consider any proposal for peace that did not recognize Southern self-rule. Though few took him seriously, Gilmer would come up with an eleventh-hour scheme for a supranational assembly—a "diet"—designed to maintain Confederate authority in the South, Union authority in the North.[6]

Robert Barnwell Rhett played a prominent part in the deliberations of the Provisional Confederate Congress in Montgomery, as a delegate from the Palmetto State. A faction promoted his presidential ambitions, but the man who had done so much to pave the way for secession found himself passed over. He and other "fire-eaters" discovered that their services were not in demand, the new Confederacy turning to conservatives for leadership. Throughout the war Rhett was a thorn in the side of Jefferson Davis. From the pages of the *Mercury* he blamed the administration for every setback.

Even after final Confederate defeat, independence was still "certain of accomplishment if the Southern People will it," according to Rhett. The

Columbia, S.C., on fire. Town Hall on the right.

South lay prostrate, but he spoke with the confidence of 1851. The old fire-brand would go to his grave convinced that "we must be separate as a people if we are to be free."[7]

━━━━━━

On the morning of February 16, 1865 federal artillery unlimbered on the west bank of the Congaree River and threw three hundred and twenty-five rounds of shot and shell into Columbia. The battle for the city had become little more than a skirmish. To slow Sherman's advance Confederates had already burned the covered span that crossed the river at Gervais Street and would destroy bridges over the Broad and Saluda as well. To avoid capture, what remained of the Southern army evacuated that night. Around daylight on the seventeenth, Mayor Thomas Jefferson Goodwyn, fretting for the safety of his city, hurried to Town Hall to raise a white flag. He and three aldermen then rode by carriage to meet the enemy.

At noon General Sherman, with his staff, galloped down Richardson Street, reigning in under that surrender flag at Town Hall. Columbia was his. Within hours fires would break out nearby. Fed by cotton and fanned by high winds, the conflagration reduced the hall, the old capitol and much of the city to smoldering ruins.

America's Third Republic had arrived.[8]

Notes

Notes to Portrait One—Thomas Cooper

1. Russell Kirk, *John Randolph of Roanoke: A Study in American Politics* (Indianapolis: 1978), p. 213.
2. Antebellum Columbia is described in Helen Kohn Hennig, ed., *Columbia Capital City of South Carolina 1786–1936* (Columbia: 1936); Robert Mills, *Statistics of South Carolina* (Charleston: 1826); Staff of the South Caroliniana Library and the Institute for Southern Studies, *A Columbia Reader 1786–1986* (Columbia: n.d.); J. F. Williams, *Old and New Columbia* (Columbia: 1929).
3. *Columbia Telescope*, 6 July 1827.
4. Ibid., 29 June 1827.
5. *Charleston Mercury*, 7 July 1827; Dumas Malone, *The Public Life of Thomas Cooper, 1783–1839* (Columbia: 1961), pp. 307–308.
6. Thomas Pettigrew Davis, "Thomas Cooper: Champion of the First Amendment" (Master's thesis, University of South Carolina, 1976), p. 7; Malone, *Cooper*, p. 259; Undated notes (Colyer Meriwether Collection, University of South Carolina).
7. Malone, *Cooper*, pp. 4–7.
8. Ibid., pp. 10–31, passim.
9. Ibid., pp. 34–52, passim and 67–68.
10. Ibid., pp. 30–31, 70–75 and 79.
11. Ibid., pp. 81–82 and 91–92.
12. Ibid., pp. 150–162, 174–175, 191 and 198–208; Davis, "Cooper," p. 40; Malone, *Cooper*, pp. 225–228, 234, 237 and 241–243.
13. Daniel Walker Hollis, *University of South Carolina*, 2 vols. (Columbia: 1951), vol. 1: *South Carolina College*, pp. 74–75; Malone, *Cooper*, pp. 19–21, 284 and 288–290.
14. Hollis, *College*, pp. 76–77, 88–91 and 101–102; Malone, *Cooper*, pp. 279–280.
15. Ibid., pp. 261–264; *Charleston Mercury*, 8 December 1832; Malone, *Cooper*, pp. 294–295; Hollis, *College*, p. 108; Davis, "Cooper," p. 12; Malone, *Cooper*, p. 392; South Carolina College was arguably a Presbyterian institution during these years. See Robert Ritholz, "The State University in the Age of the College: Cooper, Tappan and the Development of the Concept of the State University Before the Civil War" (Master's thesis, University of Wisconsin, 1975).

16. *Columbia Telescope*, 13 July 1827.

17. Henry H. Simms, *Life of John Taylor* (Richmond: 1932), pp. 61–62; Robert E. Shalhope, *John Taylor of Caroline: Pastoral Republican* (Columbia: 1980), p. 84.

18. M. E. Bradford, *Founding Fathers: Brief Lives of the Framers of the United States Constitution* (Lawrence, Kansas: 1994), pp. 16–20 and 33–35; Simms, *Taylor*, p. 47.

19. Bernard Bailyn, *The Ideological Origins of the American Revolution* (Cambridge: 1992), pp. 34–35; David L. Jacobson, ed., *The English Libertarian Heritage* (San Francisco: 1994), pp. 51–56 and 71; John Taylor, *Tyranny Unmasked* (Indianapolis: 1992), p. x.

20. Simms, *Taylor*, pp. 4–15; Shalhope, *Taylor*, pp. 13–28; Taylor, *Tyranny,* pp. ix–x.

21. Simms, *Taylor*, pp. 25–26.

22. Shalhope, *Taylor,* pp. 27–28, 31 and 108–109.

23. Merrill Jensen, *The New Nation: A History of the United States During the Confederation* (New York: 1958), p. 177 and 423–424; Alfred H. Kelly and Winfred A. Harbison, *The American Constitution: Its Origins and Development* (New York: 1970), p. 101; Henry Steele Commager, ed., *Documents of American History* (New York: 1968), pp. 111–116.

24. Kelly, *Constitution,* p. 111; Joseph L. Davis, *Sectionalism in American Politics 1774–1787* (Madison, Wisconsin: 1977), pp. 10 and 167.

25. Carl Van Doren, *The Great Rehearsal: The Story of the Making and Ratifying of the Constitution of the United States* (New York: 1948), pp. 3 and 6; Jensen, *New Nation,* pp. 29, 43, 50–51 and 59.

26. Commager, *Documents,* pp. 132–134.

27. Van Doren, *Rehearsal,* pp. 15, 34 and 63.

28. Kelly, *Constitution*, pp. 122–123; Van Doren, *Rehearsal*, pp. 53 and 72–74; Kelly, *Constitution,* pp. 129–131; United States Constitution, Article V.

29. Van Doren, *Rehearsal,* pp. 91–94; Bradford, *Fathers,* p. 44; Van Doren, *Rehearsal*, pp. 47 and 94–96.

30. Ibid., pp. 78 and 155–156; Bradford, *Fathers*, p. 203.

31. Van Doren, *Rehearsal,* pp. 160–162.

32. Ibid., p. 96; Alexander Hamilton, James Madison and John Jay, *The Federalist* (Cambridge: 1960), p. 152; Kelly, *Constitution,* p. 152.

33. Bailyn, *Origins,* pp. 335 and 344; Herbert J. Storing, ed., *The Anti-Federalist: Writings By the Opponents of the Constitution* (Chicago: 1985), p. 324.

34. Hamilton, *Federalist*, p. 239; Storing, *Anti-Federalist,* pp. 220–221; Hamilton, *Federalist,* pp. 230–231, 283 and 333.

35. Ibid., pp. 148–149; Shalhope, *Taylor,* pp. 53–54 and 55.

36. Simms, *Taylor*, pp. 47–48.

37. Taylor, *Tyranny*, pp. xi–xii.

38. Simms, *Taylor*, p. 62; Shalhope, *Taylor*, pp. 96–98; Simms, *Taylor*, pp. 70–71; Shalhope, *Taylor*, p. 95.

39. James Morton Smith, *Freedom's Fetters: The Alien and Sedition Laws and American Civil Liberties* (Ithaca, New York: 1956), p. 21; Commager, *Documents,* pp. 175–178.

40. Malone, *Cooper*, pp. 104–106, 111, 112–116 and 119.

41. Ibid., p. 127; Smith, *Fetters*, pp. 320 and 321; Malone, *Cooper*, pp. 120–122.

42. Ibid., p. 119; Davis, "Cooper," p. 28; Malone, *Cooper,* pp. 136, 148 and 172–173.

43. Davis, "Cooper," p. 34.

44. Commager, *Documents*, p. 183; Simms, *Taylor*, pp. 76–77 and 85–87.

45. Commager, *Documents*, pp. 178–182.

46. Ibid., pp. 184–185; Kelly, *Constitution,* pp. 211–212; Commager, *Documents,* p. 184.

47. William W. Freehling, *Prelude to Civil War: The Nullification Controversy in South Carolina, 1816–1836* (New York: 1992), pp. 208 and 209.

48. Thomas Jefferson, *The Writings of Thomas Jefferson* (Washington, D.C.: 1903), vol. 10, p. 302.

49. Commager, *Documents,* pp. 186–188.

50. Taylor, *Tyranny,* p. 257.

51. Hugh A. Garland, *The Life of John Randolph of Roanoke* (New York: 1853), pp. 129–141; William Cabell Bruce, *John Randolph of Roanoke, 1773–1833* (New York: 1922), vol. 1, pp. 149–153.

52. Ibid., pp. 154–155 and 565.

53. Garland, *Randolph,* pp. 7–11 and 24–28.

54. Ibid., pp. 91–92 and 370–371.

55. Kirk, *Randolph,* p. 132; Garland, *Randolph,* pp. 300–301; Bruce, *Randolph,* p. 591.

56. Ibid., p. 409; Simms, *Taylor,* pp. 205–206; Bruce, *Randolph,* p. 486.

57. Shalhope, *Taylor,* p. 206.

58. Bruce, *Randolph,* p. 431; Paul C. Bartholomew, *Summaries of Leading Cases on the Constitution* (Totowa, New Jersey: 1966), p. 163; Simms, *Taylor,* pp. 181–189.

59. Taylor, *Tyranny,* p. 208.

60. Simms, *Taylor,* pp. 179–180; Walter Kirk Wood, "The Union of the States: A Study of Radical Whig-Republican Ideology and Its Influence upon the Nation and the South, 1776–1861" (Ph.D. dissertation, University of South Carolina, 1978), p. 451.

61. Kirk, *Randolph,* p. 137.

62. Charleston *Courier,* 1 September 1827, 10 September 1827 and 15 September 1827; Malone, *Cooper,* pp. 312–314; Hollis, *College,* p. 106.

63. *Charleston Mercury,* 15 August 1827 and 21 August 1827. "Old 76" writing in the Charleston *City Gazette* of 16 August 1827 claims to discern collusion among the disunionists.

64. Ibid., 1 November 1827; Malone, *Cooper,* pp. 320–321.

Notes to Portrait Two—Robert Barnwell Rhett

1. Laura A. White, *Robert Barnwell Rhett: Father of Secession* (Gloucester, Massachusetts: 1965), p. 54.

2. Freehling, *Nullification,* p. 138; White, *Rhett,* p. 14; Freehling, *Nullification,* pp. 143–144.

3. White, *Rhett,* pp. 15–16; Freehling, *Nullification,* pp. 126 and 138–139; White, *Rhett,* p. 16; Benjamin F. Perry, *Reminiscences of Public Men* (Greenville, South Carolina: 1889), pp. 200–201; White, *Rhett,* pp. 15–16.

4. Ibid., pp. 4–6, 28, 32, 34n, and 101–102.

5. John B. Edmunds, Jr., *Francis W. Pickens and the Politics of Destruction* (Chapel Hill, North Carolina: 1986), p. 71; White, *Rhett,* pp. 100–102.

6. Ibid., pp. 6–8.

7. Freehling, *Nullification,* pp. 90–91 and 120–121. The text of the South Carolina Constitution of 1790 (in effect 1791–1865) may be found in J. H. Easterly, ed., *Basic Documents of South Carolina History* (Columbia: 1952).

8. Freehling, *Nullification,* pp. 26–27, 36 and 193–196.

9. Bruce, *Randolph,* pp. 233–237; Garland, *Randolph,* p. 311; Simms, *Taylor,* p. 126.

10. Commager, *Documents,* pp. 209–211; Kirk, *Randolph,* p. 266.

11. Freehling, *Nullification,* pp. 94–95; Bruce, *Randolph,* pp. 61 and 492.

12. Garland, *Randolph,* pp. 172–173.

13. John C. Calhoun, *A Disquisition on Government and Selections from the Discourse,* ed. by C. Gordon Post (New York: 1953), p. 101.

14. Freehling, *Nullification,* pp. 132 and 167–170.

15. Wood, "Ideology," p. 376; Freehling, *Nullification*, pp. 233–234; Wood, "Ideology," p. 549.

16. White, *Rhett*, pp. 17, 18 and 21.

17. Ibid., pp. 21–22.

18. Ibid., p. 22; Freehling, *Nullification*, pp. 235 and 254.

19. White, *Rhett*, p. 24; Rhett's place in the republican tradition is admirably presented in John C. Roberson "The Foundations of Southern Nationalism: Charleston and the Lowcountry, 1847–1861" (Ph.D. dissertation, University of South Carolina, 1991); Freehling, *Nullification*, pp. 235 and 252–253.

20. Ibid., pp. 260–261.

21. Commager, *Documents*, pp. 261–262; Freehling, *Nullification*, p. 264.

22. Margaret L. Coit, *John C. Calhoun: American Portrait* (Boston: 1950), p. 238; Freehling, *Nullification*, p. 265; Coit, *Calhoun*, pp. 242 and 245.

23. Commager, *Documents*, pp. 262–268; Freehling, *Nullification*, pp. 267 and 284–286; Coit, *Calhoun*, p. 247.

24. Freehling, *Nullification*, pp. 286–287 and 293.

25. Ibid., pp. 265 and 290.

26. Ibid., pp. 264, 275 and 277–278.

27. Ibid., pp. 292–293; Coit, *Calhoun*, p. 258; Freehling, *Nullification*, p. 295; White, *Rhett*, pp. 26–27.

28. John Belton O'Neall, *Biographical Sketches of the Bench and Bar of South Carolina* (Charleston: 1859), vol. II, p. 16.

29. Alexis de Tocqueville, *Democracy in America*, ed. by J. P. Mayer, trans. by George Lawrence (Garden City, New York: 1969), p. 392; White, *Rhett*, pp. 19–20; Freehling, *Nullification*, pp. 321–322.

30. Thomas Cooper to Joseph Priestly, 26 January 1833 (Thomas Cooper Collection, South Caroliniana Library); Robert Kenneth Faulkner, *The Jurisprudence of John Marshall* (Princeton: 1968), p. 225.

31. White, *Rhett*, pp. 28 and 32–33.

32. Ibid., pp. 34–36, 38 and 90; Edmunds, *Pickens*, p. 45.

33. White, *Rhett*, pp. 72–84, passim.

34. Ibid., pp. 88–89; Malone, *Cooper*, p. 390.

35. White, *Rhett*, p. 99.

36. Coit, *Calhoun*, p. 505; Edmunds, *Pickens*, p. 115; White, *Rhett*, p. 115.

37. Ibid., pp. 106 and 109–111; R. B. Rhett to H. Benning, 20 July 1850 (Robert Barnwell Rhett Collection, South Caroliniana Library).

38. White, *Rhett*, pp. 112–119, passim.

39. Ibid., p. 117; The text of Rhett's speech may be found in the *Charleston Mercury*, 29 April 1851. For Charleston at mid-century see Beatrice St. Julien Ravenel, *Architects of Charleston* (Charleston: 1964) and Junior League of Charleston, comp., *Historic Charleston Guidebook* (Charleston: 1971).

40. White, *Rhett*, pp. 116–120, 123 and 127–129; Edmunds, *Pickens*, p. 124; White, *Rhett*, pp. 132–133.

Notes to Portrait Three — James Henley Thornwell

1. Benjamin M. Palmer, *The Life and Letters of James Henley Thornwell* (Richmond: 1875), p. 583.

2. Ibid., pp. 477–478 and 576; James Oscar Farmer, Jr., *The Metaphysical Confederacy: James Henley Thornwell and the Synthesis of Southern Values* (Macon, Georgia: 1986), pp. 247–249.

3. Ibid., pp. 250–251; Palmer, *Thornwell*, p. 579; Farmer, *Thornwell*, pp. 249–250; Palmer, *Thornwell*, pp. 574–575 and 577–578.

4. Ibid., pp. 2–24, passim; Farmer, *Thornwell,* p. 42; Palmer, *Thornwell,* p. 22.

5. Ibid., pp. 20–21.

6. Ibid., pp. 53–55; Farmer, *Thornwell,* p. 44; Helen Kohn Hennig, *Great South Carolinians: From Colonial Days to the Confederate War* (Chapel Hill, North Carolina: 1940), p. 344; Farmer, *Thornwell,* p. 45; Palmer, *Thornwell,* pp. 71–73; James Henley Thornwell to Alexander Pegues, 19 April 1832 (James Henley Thornwell Collection, South Caroliniana Library); Farmer, *Thornwell*, pp. 44 and 46.

7. Ibid., p. 45; Palmer, *Thornwell,* p. 64.

8. Farmer, *Thornwell,* p. 47; Palmer, *Thornwell,* p. 95.

9. Ibid., pp. 105 and 112–114; Farmer, *Thornwell,* pp. 50–51; Palmer, *Thornwell,* pp. 117 and 118.

10. Farmer, *Thornwell*, pp. 51 and 69.

11. Ibid., pp. 52–54 and 61–63.

12. B. M. Palmer to J. M. Wilson, 17 May 1855 (Benjamin M. Palmer Papers, Duke University); Farmer, *Thornwell,* p. 44; Palmer, *Thornwell,* p. 566; Farmer, *Thornwell,* pp. 60 and 69; Palmer, *Thornwell,* p. 568.

13. Farmer, *Thornwell,* p. 55; Joseph G. Wardlaw, *Genealogy of the Witherspoon Family* (Yorkville, South Carolina: 1910), p. 132.

14. F. D. Jones and W. H. Mills, eds., *History of the Presbyterian Church in South Carolina Since 1850* (Columbia: 1926), p. 575; Farmer, *Thornwell,* pp. 56–57 and 57n; Palmer, *Thornwell,* pp. 548–549; Farmer, *Thornwell,* p. 57.

15. Palmer, *Thornwell,* pp. 224, 531 and 535; Farmer, *Thornwell,* p. 53; Student John Winsmith made interesting notes of Thornwell's lectures (John Christopher Winsmith Collection, South Caroliniana Library); Fitz William McMaster to G. H. McMaster, 19 August 1887 (Fitz William McMaster Collection, South Caroliniana Library).

16. Palmer, *Thornwell*, pp. 157–160, 167 and 174; Hennig, *South Carolinians,* p. 348.

17. Forrest McDonald, *Novus Ordo Seclorum: The Intellectual Origins of the Constitution* (Lawrence, Kansas: 1985), p. 51; Freehling, *Nullification,* p. 116.

18. Palmer, *Thornwell,* p. 174.

19. Ernest Trice Thompson, *Presbyterians in the South,* 3 vols. (Richmond: 1963), vol. 1: *1607–1861,* pp. 331 and 386–389.

20. James Henley Thornwell, *The Collected Writings of James Henley Thornwell,* ed. by John B. Adger and John J. Girardeau (Richmond: 1871–1873), vol. 4, pp. 384–385, 390–391 and 301–302; Philemon, vv. 1–5.

21. Thornwell, *Writings,* vol. 4, p. 393; Farmer, *Thornwell,* p. 231; Thornwell, *Writings,* vol. 4, p. 418.

22. Ibid., vol. 4, pp. 395–396.

23. Gary B. Nash and Jean R. Soderlund, *Freedom By Degrees: Emancipation in Pennsylvania and its Aftermath* (New York: 1991), pp. ix–xiii, 9, 11–13, 94–96 and 110–111.

24. de Tocqueville, *Democracy,* pp. 350 and 353.

25. Ibid., p. 353; Ulrich B. Phillips, *Life and Labor in the Old South* (Boston: 1963), pp. 185–186.

26. de Tocqueville, *Democracy,* p. 358; Phillips, *Life and Labor,* p. 339.

27. Kirk, *Randolph,* pp. 175–176, 179 and 189; Avery Craven, *Edmund Ruffin Southerner: A Study in Secession* (New York: 1932), pp. 110–111; Farmer, *Thornwell,* p. 218.

28. Thornwell, *Writings,* vol. 4, pp. 420 and 500; Farmer, *Thornwell,* p. 188; Thornwell, *Writings,* vol. 4, pp. 433 and 435.

29. Palmer, *Thornwell,* p. 305; Farmer, *Thornwell,* p. 153; Thornwell, *Writings,* vol. 4, pp. 552–556, passim.

30. Palmer, *Thornwell*, p. 545; Thornwell, *Writings*, vol. 4, pp. 382–384.

31. Farmer, *Thornwell*, p. 179; Thompson, *Presbyterians*, pp. 350–351 and 411; Farmer, *Thornwell*, p. 177.

32. Palmer, *Thornwell*, p. 286; Thompson, *Presbyterians*, pp. 530–532.

33. Farmer, *Thornwell*, pp. 187 and 246–247.

34. de Tocqueville, *Democracy*, p. 159; Simms, *Taylor*, p. 110; Wood, "Ideology," p. 480.

35. Kelly, *Constitution*, pp. 264–266; Simms, *Taylor*, p. 168; Shalhope, *Taylor*, p. 198.

36. Simms, *Taylor*, p. 167; Shalhope, *Taylor*, p. 198; Freehling, *Nullification*, p. 109; Bruce, *Randolph*, p. 448.

37. Charles S. Hyneman and Donald S. Lutz, eds., *American Political Writing During the Founding Era 1760–1805* (Indianapolis: 1983), vol. 2, p. 898; de Tocqueville, *Democracy*, p. 356.

38. David B. Chesebrough, ed., *God Ordained This War: Sermons on the Sectional Crisis, 1830–1865* (Columbia: 1991), pp. 34–35 and 40.

39. Simms, *Taylor*, p. 163.

40. Coit, *Calhoun*, pp. 361–362 and 443–444.

41. Ibid., pp. 367 and 443–444.

42. Ibid., pp. 441–443.

43. Ibid., pp. 448–449.

44. James M. McPherson, *Battle Cry of Freedom: The Civil War Era* (New York: 1988), pp. 52–55.

45. Coit, *Calhoun*, pp. 445–446 and 451–453.

46. Shalhope, *Taylor*, pp. 54–55; White, *Rhett*, pp. 115–116.

47. Coit, *Calhoun*, p. 494n.

48. Palmer, *Thornwell*, pp. 273–274 and 281–284; Farmer, *Thornwell*, pp. 183–184; Palmer, *Thornwell*, p. 343.

49. Ibid., p. 352.

50. Thornwell, *Writings*, vol. 4, pp. 403 and 414–416.

51. Palmer, *Thornwell*, p. 353; Farmer, *Thornwell*, p. 58.

52. Palmer, *Thornwell*, pp. 359 and 369.

53. Farmer, *Thornwell*, pp. 251–253.

54. Kelly, *Constitution*, pp. 369–370 and 380–383.

55. Farmer, *Thornwell*, pp. 177 and 253.

56. Ibid., p. 58; Palmer, *Thornwell*, p. 383.

57. Ibid., pp. 394 and 395–396.

58. Ibid., pp. 397, 405, 409 and 411.

59. Ibid., pp. 406 and 415–416.

60. Ibid., pp. 436–437; Wardlaw, *Genealogy*, p. 181; Palmer, *Thornwell*, pp. 439–442. The words of the inscription are taken directly from the gravestone.

61. Kelly, *Constitution*, pp. 384–389 and 391–393.

62. Kenneth M. Stampp, ed., *The Causes of the Civil War* (New York: 1991), pp. 108–109, 110, 111, 130 and 140.

63. McPherson, *Civil War*, pp. 88 and 184–186.

64. Ibid., pp. 152–153 and 202–210.

65. Dwight Lowell Dumond, *The Secession Movement 1860–1861* (New York: 1968), pp. 35–54, passim.

66. Palmer, *Thornwell,* pp. 441–442, 446 and 447.

67. Ibid., pp. 452–458, 463 and 498; Farmer, *Thornwell,* pp. 255 and 256–257.

68. Commager, *Documents*, pp. 363–365.

69. Ibid., p. 363.

70. Dumond, *Secession,* p. 271; McPherson, *Civil War*, pp. 227 and 232–233.

71. Dumond, *Secession,* pp. 117–141, passim.

72. Stampp, *Causes,* pp. 114–115 and 141.

73. W. A. Swanberg, *First Blood: The Story of Fort Sumter* (New York: 1992), pp. 16–17, 24–25; Edmunds, *Pickens,* p. 150.

74. Thornwell, *Writings*, vol. 4, pp. 511–547.

75. Ibid., p. 592. The act of secession is detailed in John A. May and Joan R. Faunt, *South Carolina Secedes* (Columbia: 1960).

76. Palmer, *Thornwell,* pp. 591–610, passim. "The State of the Country" was probably written after 11 January but before 19 January 1861. Thornwell's earliest known expression of support for the action of his state is contained in a letter to Rev. John Douglas, 31 December 1860. See Palmer, *Thornwell,* pp. 485–486.

Notes to Portrait Four — John Tyler

1. Robert Seager II, *And Tyler Too: A Biography of John and Julia Gardiner Tyler* (New York: 1963), p. 446.

2. Archie P. McDonald, ed., *A Nation of Sovereign States: Secession and War in the Confederacy* (Murfreesboro, Tennessee: 1994), pp. 12, 29, 43–46, 58–66, 71 and 83–85.

3. Commager, *Documents,* pp. 376–384.

4. Dwight Lowell Dumond, ed., *Southern Editorials on Secession* (New York: 1931), p. 414; William C. Wright, *The Secession Movement in the Middle Atlantic States* (Cranbury, New Jersey: 1973), pp. 35 and 79–80; Daniel W. Crofts, *Reluctant Confederates: Upper South Unionists in the Secession Crisis* (Chapel Hill, North Carolina: 1989), pp. 140 and 144–152, passim; McDonald, *Nation,* pp. 104 and 120.

5. Robert Gray Gunderson, *Old Gentlemen's Convention: The Washington Peace Conference of 1861* (Madison: 1961), pp. 5 and 28–29; Commager, *Documents*, pp. 374–376; Shelby Foote, *The Civil War: A Narrative* (New York: 1986), vol. 1, p. 43.

6. Lyon G. Tyler, *The Letters and Times of the Tylers* (Richmond: 1885), p. 577; Oliver P. Chitwood, *John Tyler: Champion of the Old South* (New York: 1939), pp. 432 and 434.

7. Garland, *Randolph*, pp. 237, 280 and 289–290; Seager, *Tyler,* pp. 78–79.

8. America's tenth president has been the subject of the three biographies cited here. Each presents an adequate chronology of Tyler's public life.

9. Seager, *Tyler*, pp. 1–15, passim and 204–206.

10. Ibid., p. 351.

11. Ibid., pp. 449–450.

12. Commager, *Documents,* pp. 369–371; Dumond, *Secession,* p. 161; Swanberg, *Fort Sumter,* pp. 236 and 250; Dumond, *Editorials*, p. 415.

13. Dumond, *Secession,* p. 247; Chitwood, *Tyler,* pp. 439–440 and 442–443; Seager, *Tyler,* p. 454; Jesse L. Keene, *The Peace Conference of 1861* (Tuscaloosa, Alabama: 1961), pp. 54–56.

14. Chitwood, *Tyler,* pp. 437–438 and 447.

15. Ibid., pp. 439–443; Tyler, *Letters,* pp. 624–625; Dumond, *Secession*, pp. 242–243.

16. Seager, *Tyler*, pp. 455–456; Chitwood, *Tyler,* pp. 443–444; John Tyler to James Seddon, undated [February 1861] (Tyler Peace Commission Collection, Alderman Library).

17. James Buchanan to John Tyler, 21 February 1861 (John Tyler Papers, Library of Congress).

18. Seager, *Tyler*, pp. 458–459; Chitwood, *Tyler*, p. 448; Gunderson, *Convention*, p. 84; Carl Sandburg, *Abraham Lincoln: The War Years* (New York: 1939), vol. 1, pp. 85–90.

19. Gunderson, *Convention*, p. 91; Dumond, *Secession*, pp. 252–253.

20. Tyler, *Letters*, p. 580; Chitwood, *Tyler*, p. 440; Seager, *Tyler*, pp. 456–457.

21. Dumond, *Editorials*, pp. 478–479.

22. Chitwood, *Tyler*, pp. 451–452.

23. Hudson Strode, *Jefferson Davis: American Patriot, 1808–1861* (New York: 1955), pp. 242–243; Mary Chesnut, *Mary Chesnut's Civil War*, ed. by C. Vann Woodward (New Haven: 1981), p. 722; Devereaux D. Cannon, Jr., *The Flags of the Confederacy: An Illustrated History* (Memphis: 1988), pp. 7–9; Seager, *Tyler*, p. 460.

Notes to Portrait Five — John Adams Gilmer

1. Howard Cecil Perkins, ed., *Northern Editorials on Secession* (New York: 1942), pp. 767 and 1098.

2. United States Congress, *Congressional Globe*, 36th Congress, 2nd Session, 26 January 1861, p. 580.

3. Crofts, *Reluctant Confederates*, pp. 34 and 222; John Adams Gilmer to D. H. Albright, 8 January 1861 (John A. Gilmer Collection, North Carolina State Archives).

4. *Congressional Globe*, 26 January 1861, pp. 580–583; Crofts, *Reluctant Confederates*, pp. 206–207.

5. Ibid., p. 36; Daniel W. Crofts, "A Reluctant Unionist: John Adams Gilmer and Lincoln's Cabinet," *Civil War History*, vol. 24, 1978, pp. 226–227.

6. Ibid., pp. 228–232; John G. Nicolay and John Hay, *Abraham Lincoln: A History* (New York: 1917), vol. 3, pp. 361–362; Crofts, *Reluctant Confederates*, p. 420n.

7. David C. Mearns, *The Lincoln Papers: The Story of the Collection with Selections to July 4, 1861* (New York: 1948), pp. 330–332.

8. Roy P. Basler, ed., *Collected Works of Abraham Lincoln* (New Brunswick, New Jersey: 1953), vol. 4, pp. 151–153.

9. Thurlow Weed to W. H. Seward, 9 January 1861 (William Henry Seward Papers, Rush Rhees Library); Crofts, "Reluctant Unionist," pp. 233–234; Crofts, *Reluctant Confederates*, pp. 226 and 420n; J. H. Wheeler, *Reminiscences and Memoirs of North Carolina and Eminent North Carolina Families* (n.p.: 1884), p. 193.

10. Nicolay, *Lincoln*, vol. 3, p. 364; Crofts, "Reluctant Unionist," pp. 236–239; John Adams Gilmer to Thurlow Weed, 12 January 1861 and 17 January 1861 (Thurlow Weed Papers, Rush Rhees Library); John Adams Gilmer to W. H. Seward, 7 March 1861 (William Henry Seward Papers, Rush Rhees Library).

11. John Adams Gilmer to D. H. Albright, 8 January 1861 (John A. Gilmer Collection, North Carolina State Archives); Crofts, "Reluctant Unionist," p. 240.

12. Ibid., pp. 242–243.

13. Basler, *Collected Works*, vol. 4, pp. 249–271; Crofts, "Reluctant Unionist," p. 243; McPherson, *Civil War*, p. 263.

14. Dumond, *Editorials*, pp. 252, 286 and 483–486.

15. The classic account of the "opening of hostilities" is W.A. Swanberg's *First Blood: The Story of Fort Sumter*.

16. Swanberg, *Fort Sumter*, p. 50; E. Milby Burton, *The Siege of Charleston 1861–1865* (Columbia: 1970), pp. 10–16.

17. Swanberg, *Fort Sumter*, pp. 94 and 109–110.

18. Burton, *Siege*, pp. 17–20.

19. Swanberg, *Fort Sumter*, pp. 143, 179 and 212; Cannon, *Flags*, pp. 34–35.

20. Burton, *Siege,* p. 28.

21. Crofts, *Reluctant Confederates,* pp. 257–259; John Adams Gilmer to W. H. Seward, 7 March 1861, 8 March 1861 and 12 March 1861 (William Henry Seward Papers, Rush Rhees Library).

22. Swanberg, *Fort Sumter,* pp. 222–225.

23. Ibid., pp. 230–231, 244–245, 249 and 251.

24. Commager, *Documents,* pp. 392–393.

25. McPherson, *Civil War,* pp. 271–272 and 272n.

26. Swanberg, *Fort Sumter,* pp. 270 and 279–282.

27. *The Battle of Fort Sumter and First Victory of the Southern Troops* (Charleston: 1861), pp. 31 and 32.

28. Swanberg, *Fort Sumter,* pp. 15–16; Burton, *Siege,* p. 44.

29. Ibid., pp. 44–53, passim.

30. Swanberg, *Fort Sumter,* p. 330.

31. Crofts, *Ruluctant Confederates,* p. 336.

32. Ibid., pp. 277 and 308.

33. Ibid., p. 337.

34. U.S. War Department, comp., *War of the Rebellion: A Compilation of the Official Records of the Union And Confederate Armies* (Washington, 1880–1901), ser. 3, vol. 1, pp. 67–68.

35. Hudson Strode, *Jefferson Davis: Confederate President* (New York: 1959), p. 56.

36. *Official Records,* ser. 3, vol. 1, pp. 70, 72, 76, 81, 82–83, 91–92 and 99.

37. Dumond, *Editorials,* pp. 505–506, 509–511 and 515; McPherson, *Civil War,* p. 277; Crofts, *Reluctant Confederates,* p. 337.

38. Glenn Tucker, *Zeb Vance: Champion of Personal Freedom* (Indianapolis: 1965), p. 105; Ralph A. Wooster, *The Secession Conventions of the South* (Princeton, New Jersey: 1962), p. 194.

39. Crofts, *Reluctant Confederates,* pp. 336 and 340.

40. Ibid., p. 336.

41. *Charleston Mercury,* 17 April 1861.

42. John Tyler to [Benjamin Patton], 7 May 1861 (John Tyler Papers, Manuscript Division, Library of Congress); Seager, *Tyler,* p. 459.

43. Ibid., p. 464; Chitwood, *Tyler,* p. 640.

44. McDonald, *Secession,* p. 105.

45. *Official Records,* ser. 4, vol. 1, pp. 290–291.

46. Wooster, *Conventions,* pp. 195 and 203.

47. Mark E. Neely, Jr., *The Fate of Liberty: Abraham Lincoln and Civil Liberties* (New York: 1991), pp. 5–6, 15 and 19; Glyndon Van Deusen, *William Henry Seward* (New York: 1967), p. 294.

48. McDonald, *Secession,* pp. 167–169.

49. Ibid., p. 151; Frank Moore, comp., *The Rebellion Record* (New York: 1864), pp. 254 and 258; *Official Records,* ser. 4, vol. 1, pp. 740–741.

50. [Captain] Robert E. Lee, *Recollections and Letters of General Robert E. Lee* (New York: 1904), p. 26; Larry Koger, *Black Slaveowners: Free Black Slave Masters in South Carolina 1790–1860* (Jefferson, North Carolina: 1985), pp. 189–190; *Official Records,* ser. 1, vol. 3, pp. 585–587 and ser. 1, vol. 13, pp. 500–505. For African-American support of the Confederate cause see *Black Southerners in Gray: Essays on Afro-Americans in Confederate Armies,* ed., by Richard Rollins and *Forgotten Confederates: An Anthology About Black Southerners,* ed., by Charles Kelly Barrow, et al.

51. Thompson, *Presbyterians,* p. 564; Palmer, *Thornwell,* p. 502.

52. Ibid., pp. 503–505; Farmer, *Thornwell,* pp. 278–281; Thompson, *Presbyterians,* vol. 1, p. 571 and vol. 2, p. 29; Thornwell, *Writings,* vol. 4, pp. 446–464.

Notes to the Epilogue

1. Wartime Columbia is described in Marion Brunson Lucas, *Sherman and the Burning of Columbia* (College Station, Texas: 1976), pp. 20–29.

2. Ibid., pp. 11 and 47.

3. Foote, *Civil War,* vol. 3, p. 787.

4. Palmer, *Thornwell,* pp. 513 and 521–522. "Our Danger and Our Duty" is printed in Palmer, pp. 581–590.

5. Seager, *Tyler,* pp. 469–472; Tyler, *Letters,* vol. 2, pp. 662–665.

6. Richard Current, ed., *Encyclopedia of the Confederacy* (New York: 1993), s.v. "John A. Gilmer."

7. For Rhett's wartime editorial career see Ernest B. Segars, "A Study of the *Charleston* (S.C.) *Mercury* During Robert Barnwell Rhett, Senior's Tenure As An Editorial Writer, 1861–1863" (Master's thesis, University of South Carolina, 1974); White, *Rhett,* p. 243.

8. Lucas, *Sherman,* p. 70. Oliver P. Chitwood, in his 1939 biography of John Tyler (p. 449), neatly defines three stages in American constitutional history: the First Republic (1776–1789), Second Republic (1789–1861) and Third Republic (since 1861).

Bibliography

Manuscripts and Unpublished Studies

Thomas Cooper Collection. South Caroliniana Library. University of South Carolina, Columbia.

Davis, Thomas Pettigrew. "Thomas Cooper: Champion of the First Amendment." Master's thesis, University of South Carolina, Columbia, 1976.

John Adams Gilmer Collection. North Carolina Division of Archives and History, Raleigh.

Fitz William McMaster Collection. South Caroliniana Library. University of South Carolina, Columbia.

Colyer Meriwether Collection. South Caroliniana Library. University of South Carolina, Columbia.

Benjamin M. Palmer Papers. Special Collections Library. Duke University, Durham, North Carolina.

Platte, Kenneth R. "The Religious, Political and Educational Aspects of the Thomas Cooper Controversy." Master's thesis, University South Carolina, Columbia, 1967.

Robert Barnwell Rhett Collection. South Caroliniana Library. University of South Carolina, Columbia.

Ritholz, Robert. "The State University in the Age of the College: Cooper, Tappan and the Development of the Concept of the State University Before the Civil War." Master's thesis, University of Wisconsin, Madison, 1975.

Roberson, John C. "The Foundations of Southern Nationalism: Charleston and the Lowcountry, 1847–1861." Ph.D. dissertation, University of South Carolina, Columbia, 1991.

Segars, Ernest B. "A Study of the *Charleston* (S.C.) *Mercury* During Robert Barnwell Rhett, Senior's Tenure As An Editorial Writer, 1861–1863." Master's thesis, University of South Carolina, Columbia, 1974.

William Henry Seward Papers. Department of Rare Books and Special Collections. Rush Rhees Library. University of Rochester, Rochester, New York.

James Henley Thornwell Collection. South Caroliniana Library. University of South Carolina, Columbia.

John Tyler Papers. Manuscript Division. Library of Congress. Washington, D.C.

Tyler Peace Commission Collection. Alderman Library. University of Virginia, Charlottesville.

Thurlow Weed Papers. Department of Rare Books and Special Collections. Rush Rhees Library. University of Rochester, Rochester, New York.

John Christopher Winsmith Collection. South Caroliniana Library. University of South Carolina, Columbia.

Wood, Walter Kirk. "The Union of the States: A Study of Radical Whig— Republican Ideology and Its Influence upon the Nation and the South, 1776–1861." Ph.D. dissertation, University of South Carolina, Columbia, 1978.

Newspapers

Charleston *City Gazette*, 1827.

Charleston *Courier*, 1827.

Charleston Mercury, 1827, 1832, 1851, 1861.

Columbia Telescope, 1827.

Published Primary Sources

The Battle of Fort Sumter and First Victory of the Southern Troops. Charleston, 1861.

Calhoun, John C. *A Disquisition on Government and Selections from the Discourse.* Edited by C. Gordon Post. New York, 1953.

Chesebrough, David B., ed. *God Ordained This War: Sermons on the Sectional Crisis, 1830–1865.* Columbia, South Carolina, 1991.

Chesnut, Mary. *Mary Chesnut's Civil War.* Edited by C. Vann Woodward. New Haven, 1981.

———. *The Private Mary Chesnut: The Unpublished Civil War Diaries.* Edited by C. Vann Woodward and Elisabeth Mahlenfeld. New York, 1984.

Commager, Henry Steele, ed. *Documents of American History.* New York, 1968.

de Tocqueville, Alexis. *Democracy in America.* Edited by J. P. Mayer. Translated by George Lawrence. Garden City, New York, 1969.

Dumond, Dwight Lowell, ed. *Southern Editorials on Secession.* New York, 1931.

Easterly, J. H., ed. *Basic Documents of South Carolina History.* Columbia, 1952.

Hamilton, Alexander, James Madison, and John Jay. *The Federalist.* Cambridge, 1966.

Hyneman, Charles S., and Donald S. Lutz, eds. *American Political Writing During the Founding Era 1760–1805.* Indianapolis, 1983.

Jacobsen, David L., ed. *The English Libertarian Heritage.* San Francisco, 1994.

Jefferson, Thomas. *The Writings of Thomas Jefferson.* 20 volumes. Edited by Andrew A. Lipscomb. Washington, D.C., 1903.

Lincoln, Abraham. *Collected Works of Abraham Lincoln.* Edited by Roy P. Basler. New Brunswick, New Jersey, 1953.

Mearns, David C. *The Lincoln Papers: The Story of the Collection with Selections to July 4, 1861.* New York, 1948.

Mills, Robert. *Statistics of South Carolina.* Charleston, 1826.

Moore, Frank, comp. *The Rebellion Record.* New York, 1864.

Nichols, George Ward. "Sherman's Great March." *Harper's New Monthly Magazine.* 31 (1865).

Palmer, Benjamin M. *The Life and Letters of James Henley Thornwell.* Richmond, 1875.

Perkins, Howard Cecil, ed. *Northern Editorials on Secession.* New York, 1942.

Stampp, Kenneth M., ed. *The Causes of the Civil War.* New York, 1991.

Storing, Herbert J., ed. *The Anti-Federalist: Writings By the Opponents of the Constitution.* Chicago, 1985.

Taylor, John. *Tyranny Unmasked.* Edited by F. Thornton Miller. Indianapolis, 1992.

Thornwell, James Henley. *The Collected Writings of James Henley Thornwell.* 4 volumes. Edited by John B. Adger and John J. Girardeau. Richmond, 1871–1873.

United States Congress. *Congressional Globe.* Thirty-sixth Congress, Second Session. Washington, D.C., 1861.

United States War Department, comp. *War of the Rebellion: Official Records of the Union and Confederate Armies.* 128 volumes. Washington, D.C., 1880–1901.

Secondary Sources

Bailyn, Bernard. *The Ideological Origins of the American Revolution.* Cambridge, 1992.

Barrow, Charles Kelly, J. H. Segars and R. B. Rosenburg, eds. *Forgotten Confederates: An Anthology About Black Southerners.* Atlanta, 1995.

Bartholomew, Paul C. *Summaries of Leading Cases on the Constitution.* Totowa, New Jersey, 1966.

Biographical Directory of the American Congress, 1774–1927. Washington, D.C., 1928.

Bradford, M. E. *Founding Fathers: Brief Lives of the Framers of the United States Constitution.* Lawrence, Kansas, 1994.

Bruce, William Cabell. *John Randolph of Roanoke, 1773–1833.* New York, 1922.

Burton, E. Milby. *The Siege of Charleston 1861–1865.* Columbia, South Carolina, 1970.

Cannon, Devereaux D., Jr. *The Flags of the Confederacy: An Illustrated History.* Memphis, 1988.

Chitwood, Oliver P. *John Tyler: Champion of the Old South.* New York, 1939.

Coit, Margaret. *John C. Calhoun, American Portrait.* Boston, 1950.

Craven, Avery. *Edmund Ruffin, Southerner: A Study in Secession.* New York, 1932.

Crofts, Daniel W. "A Reluctant Unionist: John Adams Gilmer and Lincoln's Cabinet." *Civil War History*, 24 (1978).

———. *Reluctant Confederates: Upper South Unionists in the Secession Crisis.* Chapel Hill, North Carolina, 1989.

Current, Richard, ed. *Encyclopedia of the Confederacy.* New York, 1993.

Davis, Joseph. *Sectionalism in American Politics, 1774–1787.* Madison, 1977.

Davis, William C. *"A Government of Our Own:" The Making of the Confederacy.* New York, 1994.

Dumond, Dwight Lowell. *The Secession Movement, 1860–1861.* New York, 1968.

Edmunds, John B., Jr. *Francis W. Pickens and the Politics of Destruction.* Chapel Hill, North Carolina, 1986.

Fant, Christie Zimmerman. *The State House of South Carolina: An Illustrated Historic Guide.* Columbia, 1970.

Farmer, James Oscar, Jr. *The Metaphysical Confederacy: James Henley Thornwell and the Synthesis of Southern Values.* Macon, Georgia, 1986.

Faulkner, Robert Kenneth. *The Jurisprudence of John Marshall.* Princeton, 1968.

Foote, Shelby. *The Civil War: A Narrative.* 3 volumes. New York, 1986.

Freehling, William W. *Prelude to Civil War: The Nullification Controversy in South Carolina, 1816–1836.* New York, 1992.

——— and Craig M. Simpson, eds. *Secession Debated: Georgia's Showdown in 1860.* New York, 1992.

Garland, Hugh A. *The Life of John Randolph of Roanoke*. New York, 1853.

Genovese, Eugene D. "James Thornwell and Southern Religion." *Southern Partisan*, Summer 1987.

Gunderson, Robert Gray. *Old Gentlemen's Convention: The Washington Peace Conference of 1861*. Madison, 1961.

Hennig, Helen Kohn, ed. *Columbia, Capital City of South Carolina, 1786–1936*. Columbia, 1936.

———. *Great South Carolinians From Colonial Days to the Confederate War*. Chapel Hill, North Carolina, 1940.

Hollis, Daniel Walker. *University of South Carolina*. 2 volumes. Columbia, 1951.

Jensen, Merrill. *The New Nation: A History of the United States During the Confederation*. New York, 1958.

Johnson, Allen, and Dumas Malone, eds. *Dictionary of American Biography*. New York, 1960.

Jones, F. D., and W. H. Mills, eds. *History of the Presbyterian Church in South Carolina Since 1850*. Columbia, 1926.

Junior League of Charleston, comp. *Historic Charleston Guidebook*. Charleston, 1971.

Keene, Jesse L. *The Peace Conference of 1861*. Tuscaloosa, Alabama, 1961.

Kelly, Alfred, and Winfred A. Harbison. *The American Constitution: Its Origins and Development*. New York, 1970.

Kirk, Russell. *John Randolph of Roanoke: A Study in American Politics*. Indianapolis, 1978.

Koger, Larry. *Black Slaveowners: Free Black Slave Masters in South Carolina, 1790–1860*. Jefferson, North Carolina, 1985.

Lee, [Captain] Robert E. *Recollections and Letters of General Robert E. Lee*. New York, 1904.

Lucas, Marion Brunson. *Sherman and the Burning of Columbia*. College Station, Texas, 1976.

Malone, Dumas. *The Public Life of Thomas Cooper 1783–1839*. Columbia, South Carolina, 1961.

May, John A., and Joan R. Faunt. *South Carolina Secedes*. Columbia, 1960.

McDonald, Archie P., ed. *A Nation of Sovereign States: Secession and War in the Confederacy*. Murfreesboro, Tennessee, 1994.

McDonald, Forrest. *Novus Ordo Seclorum: The Intellectual Origins of the Constitution*. Lawrence, Kansas, 1985.

McPherson, James M. *Battle Cry of Freedom: The Civil War Era*. New York, 1988.

Meade, Robert D. *Patrick Henry: Practical Revolutionary.* Philadelphia, 1969.

Nash, Gary, and Jean R. Soderlund. *Freedom By Degrees: Emancipation in Pennsylvania and Its Aftermath.* New York, 1991.

Neely, Mark E. *The Fate of Liberty: Abraham Lincoln and Civil Liberties.* New York, 1991.

Nicolay, John G., and John Hay. *Abraham Lincoln: A History.* 10 volumes. New York, 1917.

O'Neall, John Belton. *Biographical Sketches of the Bench and Bar of South Carolina.* Charleston, 1859.

Perry, Benjamin F. *Reminiscences of Public Men.* Greenville, South Carolina, 1889.

Phillips, Ulrich B. *Life and Labor in the Old South.* Boston, 1963.

Ravenel, Beatrice St. Julien. *Architects of Charleston.* Charleston, 1964.

Rollins, Richard, ed. *Black Southerners in Gray: Essays on Afro-Americans in Confederate Armies.* Murfreesboro, Tennessee, 1994.

Sandburg, Carl. *Abraham Lincoln: The War Years.* New York, 1939.

Seager, Robert, II. *And Tyler Too: A Biography of John and Julia Tyler.* New York, 1963.

Shalhope, Robert E. *John Taylor of Caroline: Pastoral Republican.* Columbia, South Carolina, 1980.

Simms, Henry H. *Life of John Taylor.* Richmond, 1932.

Smith, James Morton. *Freedom's Fetters: The Alien and Sedition Laws and American Civil Liberties.* Ithaca, New York, 1956.

Staff of the South Caroliniana Library and the Institute for Southern Studies. *A Columbia Reader 1786–1986.* Columbia, n.d.

Strode, Hudson. *Jefferson Davis: American Patriot, 1808–1861.* New York, 1955.

———. *Jefferson Davis: Confederate President.* New York, 1959.

Swanberg, W. A. *First Blood: The Story of Fort Sumter.* New York, 1957.

Thompson, Ernest Trice. *Presbyterians in the South.* 3 volumes. Richmond, 1963.

Tucker, Glenn. *Zeb Vance: Champion of Personal Freedom.* Indianapolis, 1965.

Tyler, Lyon Gardiner. *Letters and Times of the Tylers.* 3 volumes. Richmond, 1884–1894.

United States Capitol Historical Society. *We the People: The Story of the United States Capitol.* Washington, D.C., 1965.

Van Deusen, Glyndon. *Thurlow Weed: Wizard of the Lobby.* Boston, 1947.

———. *William Henry Seward.* New York, 1967.

Van Doren, Carl. *The Great Rehearsal: The Story of the Making and Ratifying of the Constitution of the United States.* New York, 1948.

Walther, Eric H. *The Fire-Eaters.* Baton Rouge, 1992.

Wardlaw, Joseph G. *Genealogy of the Witherspoon Family.* Yorkville, South Carolina, 1910.

Warner, Ezra, and W. Buck Yearns. *Biographical Register of the Confederate Congress.* Baton Rouge, 1975.

Weaver, Richard M. *The Southern Tradition at Bay: A History of Postbellum Thought.* New Rochelle, 1968.

Wheeler, J. H. *Reminiscences and Memoirs of North Carolina and Eminent North Carolina Families.* n.p., 1884.

White, Laura. *Robert Barnwell Rhett: Father of Secession.* Gloucester, Massachusetts, 1965.

Williams, J. F. *Old and New Columbia.* Columbia, South Carolina, 1929.

Wooster, Ralph A. *The Secession Conventions of the South.* Princeton, 1962.

Wright, William C. *The Secession Movement in the Middle Atlantic States.* Cranbury, New Jersey, 1973.

Index